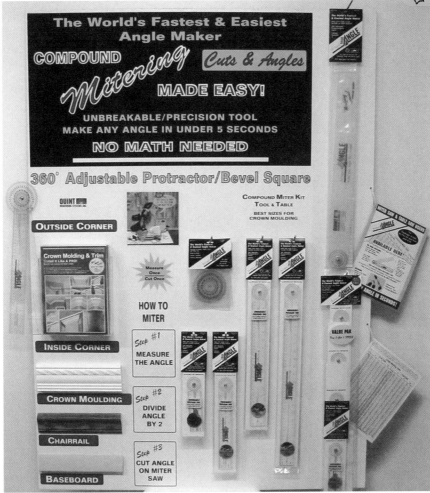

Read what our customers are saying!

Wayne, I've read many books on finish carpentry and particularly installation of crown/trim molding that claim to be for "do-it-yourselfers". Your book far surpasses anything I've seen. As an engineer myself, I can appreciate the level of detail that you provide for installing crown/trim molding. Many books promise "easy techniques" for installing molding, but the instructions are usually vague and the illustrations confusing. Not so with your book. Your instructions and illustrations are crystal clear. I've put off for years installing crown molding in our house because I was simply intimidated by it. With your book and the True Angle® tools, I now have the tools/techniques and the confidence I need to do a professional job. Thanks for a wonderful product.   Chris

Wayne, I purchased an 18 inch True Angle® tool and Crown Moulding Table. They were a great value, and proved invaluable installing the crown moulding in our 80 year old home. This was a total do-it-yourself project from start to finish. The True Angle® tool and Crown Moulding Table© made cutting the crown moulding precise and resulted in flawless joints. This was truly a case of having the right tool for the job and I have to emphasize again the cost of your tools were amazingly inexpensive.   Frank R Syracuse, NY

Wayne, I installed 5¼ inch crown in my large family room, living room and master bedroom all in 3 days! Thanks to your SIMPLE instructions and tools, I'm sure I saved thousands of dollars in carpenter's costs and gained the respect and admiration of my husband and male chauvinist friends! All my husband had to do was hold up the ends of the moldings while I nailed them into place. The look of amazement on his face when all the corners matched was priceless! If I can do it, anyone can! Thanks to your great products, I was able to beautifully upgrade my home for the Price of the materials alone. Thank you! Mary

Wayne, Thanks a million! You have saved me a lot of $$$ with your great products and directions for installing crown molding. Of all the guides and directions I've tried, yours is the only one that has worked. Dwayne T.

Wayne, I am sorry I didn't email you earlier today, but I was done so quickly I had time to install 1/4 round molding as well. Using your book Crown Molding & Trim Install It Like a Pro and True Angle® tools made short work of my crown molding project. When I started this project I thought that I would never figure out how to install the Crown Molding. I wasted 2, 12 foot pieces before I gave up. But one search engine later, I found your web site and the rest is History. Thank You for putting together such a well thought out and precise product for us do-it-yourselfers. Regards, Manny

Wayne, I now have installed crown molding in a couple of areas and it sure was nice to make every cut a good one. I tried to figure out how to cut crown molding, but after going through about 15 board feet I still had no hope of getting it right. I then purchased the set of True Angle® tools and compound miter products which made it almost too easy. Kelly D.

Wayne, I just wanted to take the time to say that you saved my life! Not really, but I don't know what I would have done without your tools and compound miter information. This was my first attempt, and I had heard some nightmare stories from both family members, and by reading on the internet about the problems with installing crown molding. I did an excellent job on my first try! My father-in-law accused me of hiring a professional! Sincerely, Jerry B.

Wayne, I spent the better part of a day trying to install some crown molding in the dining room. Well, after 4 hours and wasting about 12 feet of molding, I decided to call a professional. To my dismay, no one returned my calls. I had seen your website previously, but was really skeptical. When I received your products, I figured I would "test" it by cutting an outside corner that was consistently giving me a one inch gap at the top. I then took the two pieces upstairs for a trial fit and....I almost fell off the ladder, an outside corner without any gaps!!! I really couldn't believe it. I then proceeded to finish the rest of the room and it looks GREAT. I just had to say THANK YOU WAYNE!!!! Larry

Wayne, I received the book today and it looks great. The chapter describing how to square-up the miter saw is a much needed item since most people, not me of course ;-), don't know how or why to do that. This is the first book or document that I have seen that truly gives the novice a strong starting point and a great reference tool to becoming successful the very first time, including the little touches to finish off the project. It makes no assumptions about skill level or abilities which is a plus! Thanks again, Mike.

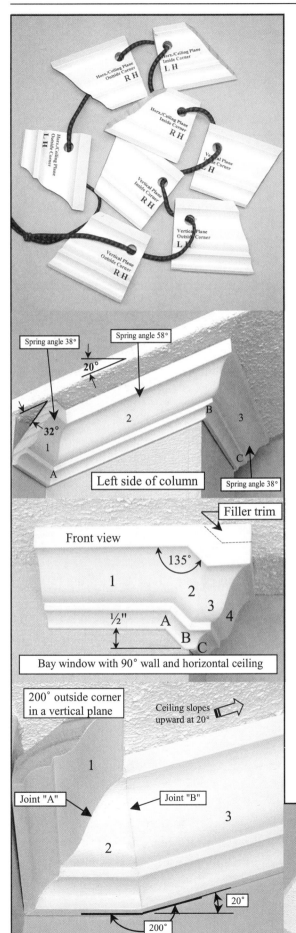

Spring angle 38°

Spring angle 58°

20°

32°

2

B

3

C

1

A

Spring angle 38°

Left side of column

Filler trim

Front view

135°

1

2

3

4

½"

A

B

C

Bay window with 90° wall and horizontal ceiling

200° outside corner in a vertical plane

Ceiling slopes upward at 20°

1

Joint "A"

Joint "B"

3

2

20°

200°

Crown Molding & Trim
Install It Like A PRO!

Master any compound miter angle.

Created and designed by
Wayne and Kathy Drake
www.compoundmiter.com
a Quint Group company

Special thanks to my editors
Richard Quint (Technical Editor)
Carol Quint
Debra Clinger
John Gardner
Ned Westerlund

Edition IA, Copyright 2003
Published and distributed exclusively by
Quint Measuring Systems, Inc. All rights reserved.
Printed in the U.S.A.

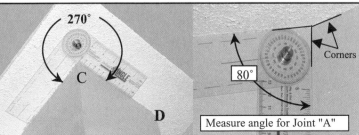

270°

C

80°

Corners

D

Measure angle for Joint "A"

HOW TO USE THIS BOOK

I have written this book with the novice *do-it-yourselfer* in mind who would like to add beauty and value to their homes. I have developed a simple 3-step method that will allow even the most inexperienced homeowner to easily cut and install crown molding and trim. Nothing you do will improve the appearance and value of your home more than beautifully installed crown molding/trim. Hiring a professional will cost 5 to 10 times more than doing it yourself. With my proven 3-step method, you will be able to easily cut and install crown/trim and save thousands of dollars.

The professional carpenter will also benefit from this book because of the simple approach I have developed for cutting crown for a cathedral ceiling. Even some of the most experienced carpenters have difficulties with cathedral ceilings.

A major portion of this book is devoted to explaining how to make certain types of turns with crown molding or trim. I have followed up with numerous examples to further demonstrate these concepts. Once you understand these simple concepts, you will be able to use your Original True Angle® tools, as well as the tables and charts included in this book, to easily make the cuts needed.

There is nothing difficult about installing crown molding or trim. All you need are the right tools and information to do the job. Complete instructions are included for both types of saws, a **miter saw** or a **compound miter saw**. I *strongly* encourage you to read this book from cover to cover before you begin making any cuts. If you can hammer a nail, you *can* Install Crown Molding & Trim Like A Pro! Become a master of compound miter cuts.

Easy 3-Step Method to Install Crown Molding & Trim

1. Measure the corner angle with your True Angle® tool.
2. Get the miter and blade tilt angles from the charts/tables in this book.
3. Set your saw and make the perfect cut.

Visit our website at www.compoundmiter.com and check out the many testimonials and project pictures that have been received from our customers.

About the Author:

Wayne Drake has been a mechanical engineer by profession since 1973. He has an extensive background in advanced mathematics and engineering graphics. He received his Bachelor of Science degree in Mechanical Engineering from Georgia Institute of Technology in Atlanta, Georgia in December 1972 and his Master of Science degree in Aeronautical Systems Engineering from the University of West Florida in 1976. His interest in cutting and installing crown molding and trim stems from his many years as a woodworking hobbyist. The event that led to the founding of www.compoundmiter.com (March 2000) was the construction of six of the large birdfeeders shown on his website and in Chapter 16 of this book. While making these as Christmas presents, he discovered, after cutting all 24 gazebo roof pieces, the birdfeeder plans had the wrong miter and blade tilt angles. He then sat down and graphically derived what is now called the Compound Miter Chart© which illustrates the relationship between corner angle and crown slope angle for a compound miter cut. Today, www.compoundmiter.com is the best and only one-stop-source for information on how to cut any compound miter angle.

Contents

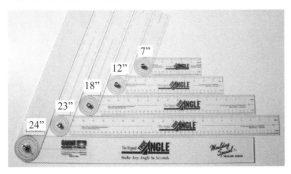

Chapter 1 – Getting Ready/Gathering Materials

Laying out your work area using The Original True Angle® tool with examples of how to estimate the amount of crown molding or trim needed.

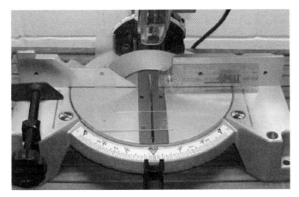

Chapter 2 – Squaring Your Saw

Before you begin any project, you must check your saw for accuracy. Most new saws have not been precisely aligned and may not be square.

Chapter 3 – Baseboards and Trim

The Baseboards and Trim chapter applies to any type of trim installed flat on a surface (usually the wall). This includes baseboards, chair rails, quarter and half-round trim, cove molding, corner molding, fireplace trim, and door and window casings.

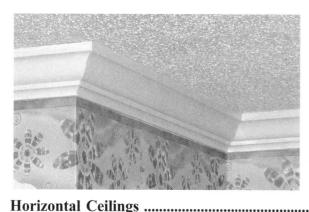

Chapter 4 – Horizontal Ceilings

There are two types of corner cuts for a horizontal ceiling — inside corners and outside corners. Detailed examples are provided with step-by-step instructions on how to cut your crown, regardless of your corner angle, using either a miter saw or a compound miter saw.

Chapter 5 – Cathedral/Vaulted Ceilings

Crown molding on a cathedral ceiling made easy. Here we will cover practically any situation you might encounter. There are several techniques demonstrated, as well as the pros and cons for each.

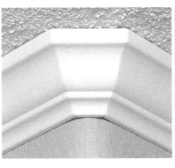 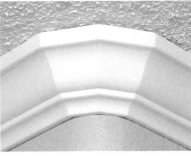

Chapter 6 – Bullnose (Radius) Corners

Bullnose corners are detailed for any corner angle and any bullnose corner radius. With the information in this chapter, you will be able to easily install your bullnose corners.

Chapter 7 – Splicing/Joining Crown or Trim

Often you will have a wall that is longer than a full length of crown/trim. Or you may have several long pieces remaining that you want to use instead of buying more full-length pieces. This chapter shows you how to best splice/join crown or trim.

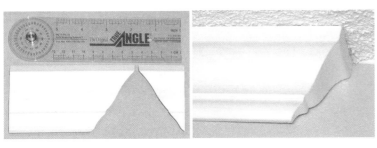

Chapter 8 – Crown Return

Occasionally, you will need to return the crown to the wall and stop, instead of continuing into a corner.

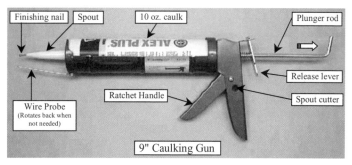

Finishing nail | Spout | 10 oz. caulk | Plunger rod
Release lever
Ratchet Handle | Spout cutter
Wire Probe (Rotates back when not needed)
9" Caulking Gun

Chapter 9 – Caulking Your Crown/Trim

Caulking your crown or trim will make the difference between a good-looking job and a fantastic-looking job. Learn the proper way to caulk.

Chapter 10 – Crown Cornices/Shelves

These decorative cornices and shelves will accent any room. Easily make cornices, shelves, shadowboxes, fireplace mantels, or other ornate items from the same crown installed in your house.

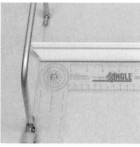

Chapter 11 – Coping

How to properly cope a joint. This chapter covers both trim that is placed flat on the wall and crown molding.

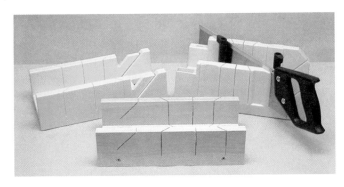

Chapter 12 – Miter Boxes

There are several types of miter boxes available. We will show you how to use these and explain some of their advantages and disadvantages.

Chapter 13 – Adjustable Miter Boxes

An interim step between the previously mentioned fixed miter boxes (Chapter 12) and the adjustable electric miter and compound miter saws (Chapters 3, 4, and 5) is the adjustable steel miter box that comes with an attached saw. I will cover two types that are available and how to use them.

Chapter 14 - Miters for Acute Corners

In today's construction architecture, many homes are built with acute corners. To cut a miter for these acute corners requires that you set your saw beyond the saw's ±45° adjustment capability. I will show you how to cut any miter for acute corners using a simple-to-build portable fence.

Chapter 15 – Flowerpots

Create any size flowerpot you want. Three sides to 20 sides (or more), any size and any wall angle you want. Cut your material with confidence. Every joint will fit perfectly. Use your scrap crown with fantastic results.

Chapter 16 – Birdhouses and Gazebos

Everyone will love these birdhouses. You can build any style imaginable. Three to 20 sides, small or large. Step-by-step instructions show you how.

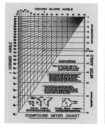 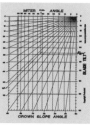

Chapter 17 – Definitions, Tables, and Charts

In this chapter, I have included all the definitions, tables, and charts that you will frequently refer to while installing your crown molding or trim. I have also included two conversion tables. One converts fractions of an inch to decimals of an inch, and the other converts roof pitch to roof slope.

Getting Ready/Gathering Materials

The first step to installing crown molding or trim is to gather your materials. You will need the usual items such as saw, hammer, nails, caulk, putty knife, etc. In addition to the usual items, you will need a set of The Original True Angle® tools (to measure corner angles), Miter Table© (for trim/crown using a miter saw), Crown Molding Table© (for horizontal ceilings), Compound Miter Chart© (for cathedral/vaulted ceilings), and/or Miter Excel Program© (available through our website). Let's start by providing information about the True Angle® and how to use it.

Using Your True Angle® Tool

The Original True Angle® is the "world's fastest, easiest angle maker." It can be used to measure any inside or outside corner from 0° to 360°. The tools are manufactured to very close tolerances, resulting in accuracy equal to or greater than any other angle-measuring tool that might cost 5 times as much. The True Angle® tools are unbreakable and carry a **lifetime free replacement warranty**.

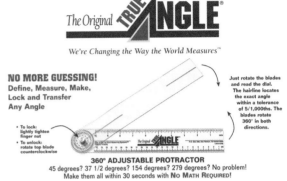

The True Angle® replaces every triangle, protractor, try square, bevel square, rafter square, framing square, combination square, or any other angle making template presently manufactured anywhere in the world. To use the tool, just place the two blades against the two surfaces you want to measure and tighten the tension nut. Then, read the angle on the scales printed directly on the tool. If you have difficulty loosening the tension nut on the True Angle®, hold the lower blade of the tool in your left hand, then rotate the upper blade counter-clockwise (CCW). All of the True Angle® tools can be purchased through our website.

Why do I need to measure my corners? Aren't they all square?

It is not uncommon to have corners out of square as much as 3°. If you are cutting 5" crown molding, a 3° error will result in a 3/8" gap in the joint. (The larger the crown, the bigger the gap.) With a true corner angle measurement, you will be able to get the exact saw settings to make the perfect cut.

Measuring an Outside Corner – (Corners that measure between 180° and 360°)

This photo shows how to measure an outside corner using the 7" True Angle®. The shorter tools are needed for corners that will not accommodate the longer tools. **Use the longest tool that will fit the corner for greatest accuracy**. The 7" True Angle® is used to measure this outside corner (photograph to the right) because of the doorframe casing to the left. To measure the corner angle, place the blades of the tool snugly against the two walls, then tighten the tension nut so the two blades

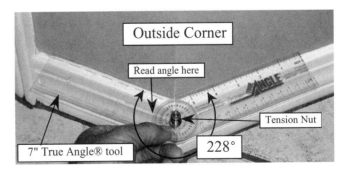

do not move. Remove the tool from the corner and read the angle at the hairline as shown. There are two angles indicated on the tool. The outer scale is for inside corners and the inner scale is for outside corners. The corner in the above picture measures 228° (outside corner).

Note: When cutting any type of crown/trim, the two indicated angles on the tool (inside or outside corner) will have the same miter and blade tilt angles found in the Miter Table© (Chapter 3), the Crown Molding Table© (Chapter 4) or the Compound Miter Chart© (Chapter 5). The only differences are in the way you place the crown/trim on your saw and in which direction you adjust your miter and/or blade tilt angles. To make it easy, just use the correct template as a guide for the type of cut you want to make (See Chapters 4 and 5 on how to make your own templates or simply purchase a set through our website).

Measuring an Inside Corner – (Corners that measure between 0° and 180°)

Here I am using my 23" True Angle® to measure an inside corner. In this example, the inside corner is 132°. For an inside corner, read the angle from the outside scale on the True Angle®.

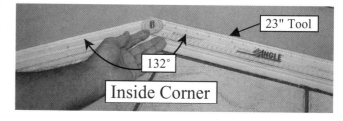

Inside Corner

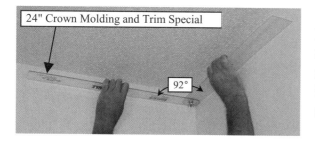

24" Crown Molding and Trim Special

I am using my 24" (heavy-duty) True Angle® Crown Molding Special to measure the angle of an inside corner. Always measure the corner angle at the location you are going to install your trim or crown. Do *not* measure 4' off the floor and use that angle for baseboards or crown.

Which True Angle® Tool Do I Need?

We offer a wide selection of True Angle® tools available on our website. The tools range in size from 7" to 96" in length. The sizes shown in the photo to the right (7" through 24") are ideally suited for trim and crown molding applications. Use the longest tool that will fit the corner. The shorter tools will be needed for those short walls that the longer tools will not fit. The larger tools (30" through 96") are great for construction/foundation layout applications, including cabinets, countertops, and flooring.

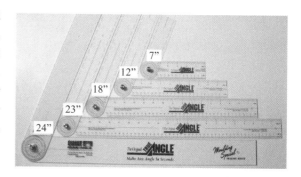

For the do-it-yourselfer, the best tools for crown molding and trim application are the 7", 12", 18", and 23" tools. These can be purchased as a **Best Value Tool Package** (get the 7" tool free), or they can be purchased individually. The 24" tool is contractor-grade, heavy-duty (blades are 0.125" thick). The Original True Angle® tool is a precision manufactured tool that has many uses. You and your family will discover hundreds of other uses for the True Angle® tools in both your workshop and around the house. My wife uses hers for sewing and crafting, while our children use theirs for schoolwork.

The minimum size we recommend is the 18" tool (unless the wall is too short for the tool). Why? When drywall is installed in your house, a metal cap is placed on the outside corner. Drywall mud is then applied to smooth the corner. If you measure an outside corner with a 7" tool, because of the corner cap and the mud, you will not have an accurate corner angle measurement of the two walls. We recommend you extend past one wall stud (typically 16" on center) to measure the corner angle. The 18" tool will take you past the first wall stud and provide a more accurate measurement of the angle between the two walls.

Try this: Place a 3' straight edge horizontally, starting on any outside (drywall) corner in your house. Now look at the straight edge and the wall about 6" to 8" from the corner. You will see approximately 1/8" to 1/4" gap between the wall and the straight edge. If you use a 7" tool to measure this corner, you will not have the true angle measurement of the walls (it will be about 3° to 4° less than the true wall angle). The 23" or 24" True Angle® tools will provide the best accuracy for outside corners. The 7" and 12" tools are ideally suited for close corners where the larger tools will not fit.

Estimating Crown Molding/Trim to Purchase

To estimate the amount of material to purchase, make a sketch of your work area using your True Angle® tool. This will not take long to do, but it could save you another trip to the building supply store because you ran out of material or you bought too much.

Measure each wall length and corner angle and place these dimensions on your sketch. To estimate how much crown/trim you need, add the lengths needed for each wall to get a total. Because there is always some scrap left over from every cut, you will need to add extra length to each piece. For trim, round the wall lengths up to the next whole inch, then add 3" for each piece. For crown, round the wall lengths up to the next whole inch and add 1.5 times the crown width to each piece (e.g., 4" crown width x 1.5 = 6" extra for each piece).

Let's do this example as though we were installing baseboard. Baseboard piece #1 would be 186"+3" = 189" (186" was obtained by rounding 185-3/8" up to the next whole inch). Continue around the room for each piece. You should get a total of 855" of trim needed. Divide 855" by 12 to get the number of feet (855÷12 = 71.25 ft.). Round 71.25' to 72'.

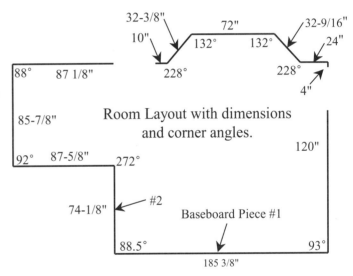
Room Layout with dimensions and corner angles.

Most crown/trim comes in 16' lengths. To obtain how many 16' pieces of trim you need, divide 72' by 16 (72÷16 = 4.5 pieces of trim). You will need to get 5 full lengths of trim. You should start on the longest wall. Try to use the long, full lengths to place on the long walls of the room and use the shorter pieces cut from the long pieces to do the shorter walls. By planning this way, you will not need to make any splices in the trim unless, of course, you have a wall longer than 16' (See Chapter 7).

If you were installing 4" crown molding, you would round each wall length up to the next inch and add 6" (4" x 1.5 = 6") to each wall length. Wall #1 would be 186"+6" = 192". The total would be 891" of 4" crown molding or 4.7 pieces of 16' crown molding. You would need to purchase 5 full 16' lengths.

Let's run through a small exercise to determine which pieces to cut from each full length of trim. Start by numbering the longest wall in your layout sketch as wall #1, then continue counter-clockwise around the room. In our example, we have a total of 12 pieces (12 walls) of trim to cut from 5 full lengths (16' lengths) of trim. Next, number each piece of trim #1 through #5. (Always start a full length of trim with the longest wall remaining.) For full-length trim piece #1, mark the back of the trim "wall piece #1". As you determine which wall pieces you are going to cut from each full length of trim/crown, mark the back of that full length of trim until all of the crown/trim is marked.

1st piece of 16' trim: Start with the longest wall. You will be able to cut wall #1.
2nd piece of 16' trim: Start with the next longest wall. That will be wall #12 and then walls #7 and #9.
3rd piece of 16' trim: From this piece, you can get walls #3, #4 and #6.
4th piece of 16' trim: Next would be wall #5, #2 and #10
5th piece of trim: The remaining walls are #8 and #11.

After all of your trim is marked, start with wall #1 (the longest wall in the room) and work your way around the room installing each piece as you go. Cut and install crown/trim piece #1 (Chapter 3). Next, install trim piece #2. Locate the full length of trim you labeled for trim piece #2 and use this one to cut #2 from. Continue around the room until all of your trim is installed.

If you are working on a tight budget and want to keep costs down, ask an employee at the building supply store if you can cut only what you need from a full-length piece (e.g., trim pieces #8 and #11). The drawback to this is, that during the installation, if you make a wrong cut or split a piece of trim while nailing, you may not have enough trim to finish the job you had planned for the weekend.

Summary and Review
How to Use The Original True Angle® Tool
Place the two blades against the surfaces you want to measure and tighten the tension nut. Then read the angle on the scale printed on the tool. To loosen the tension nut, hold the lower blade in your left hand and turn the top blade counter-clockwise. There are several sizes of True Angle® tools available (7" through 24") for crown/trim application. Use the longest tool that will fit the corner. The shorter tools will be needed for the shorter walls.

How to Layout and Plan Your Work
Here we discussed how to make a sketch of the room where you will be working. Use your True Angle® to measure all the corner angles. To get the estimated length for each wall, round the wall length up to the next whole inch, then add 3" for trim, or for crown, 1.5 times the crown width. Add all of the estimated wall lengths to get the total amount of crown/trim needed. If you need crown longer than 16', call or visit some of your local building supply stores to see if they have longer lengths.

How to Mark Each Piece of Crown/Trim
Here we covered how to take each full length of crown/trim and decide which wall piece we will cut from it. Mark the first full length piece of crown/trim for the longest wall, then determine which of the shorter walls can be cut from the remainder of that first full piece. Do this until all of the full lengths of crown/trim are marked for the proper wall. Start installing the crown/trim on the longest wall. It is best to install your crown/trim sequentially as you work your way around the room either clockwise (CW) or counter-clockwise.

Squaring Your Saw

One of the most important, and often overlooked, things to do before starting your crown/trim project is to check the square and accuracy of your saw. I often get emails from customers who are having a difficult time making good compound miter joints. They have followed my instructions, but the joints just do not fit. This is often caused by not squaring your saw before you start. Since all compound miter joints are cut as a mirror image of each other, for each degree the saw is out of square, the joint has twice the error. It is not uncommon for the fence on your saw to be out of square as much as 3°. If you are using 5" crown molding, 3° out of square will result in a 3/8" gap in the joint. In this chapter, I will be covering the basic process of squaring a saw, using my 10" compound miter saw as an example.

Saw Adjustment Locations

Let's start by briefly describing the general locations of the adjustments. Check your owner's manual to find the location of all of your adjustments. Your saw may be different, but the adjustment process will be the same. Squaring the blade tilt on a compound miter saw will be done with the blade tilt stops, the blade tilt scale, and scale pointers. The miter will be adjusted using the fence adjustment bolts and the miter angle pointer. Be sure to check the overall tightness of all of the nuts and bolts on your saw. Check to make sure the blade will rise up and down smoothly. (If you have a miter saw, check to make sure the saw blade is square with the miter table.)

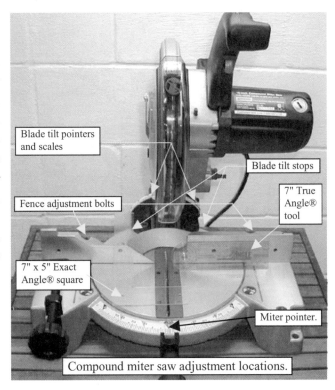

Blade tilt pointers and scales
Blade tilt stops
Fence adjustment bolts
7" True Angle® tool
7" x 5" Exact Angle® square
Miter pointer.

Compound miter saw adjustment locations.

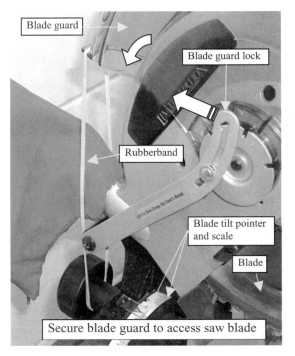

Blade guard
Blade guard lock
Rubberband
Blade tilt pointer and scale
Blade

Secure blade guard to access saw blade

Always unplug your saw before making any adjustments! Follow your saw manufacturer's safety procedures carefully to avoid injury.

Release the blade guard lock and rotate the blade guard up and out of your way to gain free access to the saw blade. The blade guard is spring-loaded and will not stay in place. Here, I have used a rubber band to secure the blade guard. We will first square the blade tilt, then square the miter.

Square the Blade-tilt

You should use your Exact Angle® square or your 7" True Angle® tool. (A full line of Exact Angle® squares is available on our website.) Place your square as shown in the photograph to the right. Make sure the square is not resting on a saw tooth and that the base of the square is resting on the miter table. There are two adjustable blade tilt stops for a compound miter saw that must be checked. One of these is the 0° blade tilt adjustment. Adjust the 0° blade tilt stop until the saw blade has full contact with your 90° square.

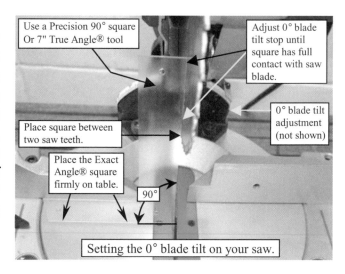

Use a Precision 90° square Or 7" True Angle® tool

Adjust 0° blade tilt stop until square has full contact with saw blade.

0° blade tilt adjustment (not shown)

Place square between two saw teeth.

Place the Exact Angle® square firmly on table.

90°

Setting the 0° blade tilt on your saw.

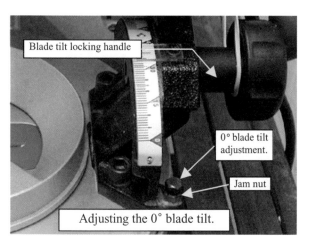

Blade tilt locking handle

0° blade tilt adjustment.

Jam nut

Adjusting the 0° blade tilt.

First loosen the blade tilt locking handle and tilt the blade all the way against the 0° blade tilt stop. (Leave the blade tilt locking handle loose.) Now check your 90° square to see if it is resting firmly against the saw blade. If there is a gap between the top of the square and your saw blade, the blade tilt stop needs to be adjusted so that the saw blade tilts more to the left. Loosen the jam nut on your 0° blade tilt adjustment and turn the adjustment counter-clockwise until the saw blade is in full contact with your square. If the gap is between the bottom edge of your saw blade and your square, turn the blade tilt adjustment clockwise. When finished, lock the blade tilt jam nut and recheck the square to ensure it is in full contact with the miter table and your saw blade. If you are using a miter saw (blade will not tilt), you do not have blade tilt stops, but there will be some adjustments for squaring your saw. Check your saw manual. It is important that the saw blade makes a true 90° angle with the miter table.

Adjusting Blade-tilt Scales and Pointers

You are now ready to set the blade tilt pointers so they read the correct angle. Loosen the screw that holds the pointer, then align it with the 0° mark on the scale. If there is not enough adjustment in the pointer to align the 0° mark, loosen the scale to make further adjustments. When finished, you should get a perfect 90° angle between the saw blade and the miter table with the saw head resting on the 0° stop. Both pointers (left and right side) should be in perfect alignment with the 0° mark on the blade tilt scales. On a compound miter saw, there are usually two blade tilt pointers and two blade tilt scales. All will need to be set. Now move the blade tilt to the 45° blade tilt stop and check the angle between the saw blade and the miter table. Adjust the 45° blade tilt stop if necessary.

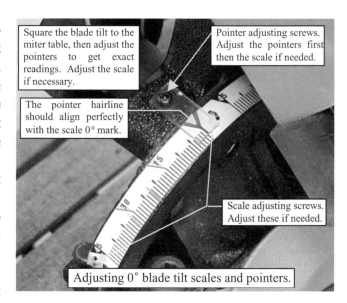

Square the blade tilt to the miter table, then adjust the pointers to get exact readings. Adjust the scale if necessary.

Pointer adjusting screws. Adjust the pointers first then the scale if needed.

The pointer hairline should align perfectly with the scale 0° mark.

Scale adjusting screws. Adjust these if needed.

Adjusting 0° blade tilt scales and pointers.

Square the Fence

Now that you have the blade tilt square with the table, you are ready to square the fence with the saw blade. Set the blade tilt in the 0° position and make sure the miter-indexing lever is set in the 0° position. Lower the saw head down so the blade is through the miter table. My 10" compound miter saw has a lock pin (not shown) to hold the saw in the down position for storage or transportation. Check your saw manual for the same feature and lock the saw blade down. Place your Exact Angle® square or your 7" True Angle® flat on the miter table against the saw blade and the fence. Make sure your square is not resting on any of the saw blade teeth. Hold the square firmly against the saw blade, then

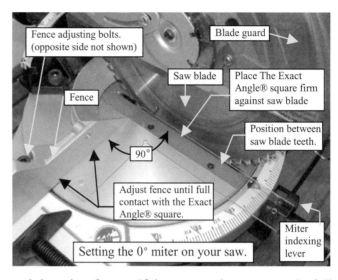

Fence adjusting bolts. (opposite side not shown)

Blade guard

Saw blade

Fence

Place The Exact Angle® square firm against saw blade

Position between saw blade teeth.

90°

Adjust fence until full contact with the Exact Angle® square.

Miter indexing lever

Setting the 0° miter on your saw.

check to see if there are any gaps between the square and the miter fence. If the square does not rest in full contact with the fence, loosen the fence adjusting bolts and align the fence. When finished, lock the fence adjusting bolts and recheck the square of the saw blade and the miter fence.

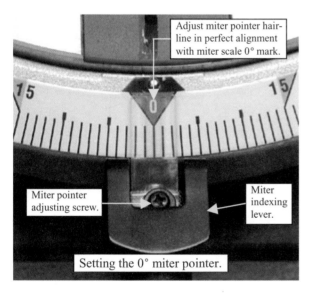

Adjust miter pointer hair-line in perfect alignment with miter scale 0° mark.

15   15

Miter pointer adjusting screw.

Miter indexing lever.

Setting the 0° miter pointer.

The last adjustment is to set the miter pointer. Loosen the miter pointer screw and adjust the pointer hairline so that it is in perfect alignment with the miter angle scale as shown. If you need more adjustment, check your saw manual for any additional adjustment locations.

Tighten all adjusting screws and bolts and recheck both the 0° blade tilt and the 0° miter setting with your Exact Angle® square. If both are still set to 90°, you are finished.

Congratulations! You have now set the square of your saw and are ready to start cutting your crown molding or trim.

Summary and Review

You **must** check the square of your saw before you begin. This is very important. There are a lot of differences between saws that are on the market. Check your saw manual for specific instructions. However, all saws will be squared in much the same manner. First square the saw blade (90°) to the miter table, then adjust the pointer hairlines to read 0° blade tilt. Square the miter fence to the saw blade and adjust the miter pointer hairline to the 0° miter setting. This simple alignment process will guarantee perfect miter joints for all your crown molding or trim work.

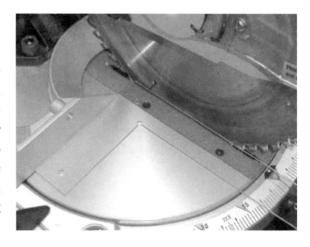

Baseboards and Trim

In this chapter, we will address how to cut and install trim which is placed flat on the wall. We will use both a miter saw (blade will not tilt) and a compound miter saw. This type of trim includes baseboards, chair rails, quarter and half-round trim, cove molding, corner molding, fireplace trim, and door and window casings.

Trim is most often installed using horizontal turns and will either form an inside or an outside corner, such as when you are installing baseboards or chair rails. Trim can also turn vertically when you are trimming out a staircase or other areas that run at an incline or sloping angle. Let's start by demonstrating how to cut horizontal turns using a miter saw. Always check the square of your saw before you begin cutting (Chapter 2). As we work our way through these examples, you should make yourself a template for each example. Cut the templates about 3" long and label each one as shown. Using your set of templates will prevent you from cutting your trim wrong.

Using a Miter Saw
Horizontal Turns

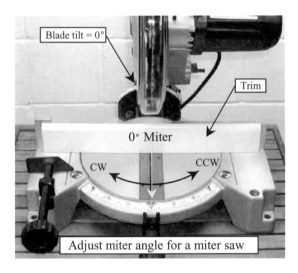

Blade tilt = 0°

Trim

0° Miter

CW   CCW

Adjust miter angle for a miter saw

If you are using a miter saw to cut your trim, stand your trim up with the back of the trim placed firmly against the saw fence. The saw I am using here is a compound miter saw. A miter saw operates the same when you set the blade tilt to 0° and only adjust the miter angle either clockwise or counter-clockwise.

There are two common problems when using a miter saw. Often the trim is taller than the fence, or in the case of very large trim, the saw blade will not cut all the way through the trim. In the case of the fence being too short for the trim, you can attach a straight board to the fence to extend the height. The back (top and bottom) of the trim must rest firmly against the fence. If your saw will not cut through the trim, use a larger saw or smaller trim.

Outside Corner Left-hand Piece

Using your True Angle® tool, measure the corner angle where you want to install the trim. Then obtain the miter angle setting you need from the Miter Table© located at the end of this chapter. For the outside corner left-hand piece, rotate your miter saw counter-clockwise to the miter angle for the corner you measured. Here I have set my miter for an outside corner cut for the left-hand piece. Let's say, as an example, the corner you measured is 268°. From the Miter Table©, for a corner angle of 268°, you get a miter angle of 44°. Set your saw as shown and make your cut.

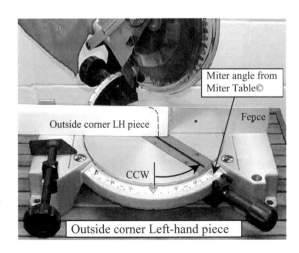

Miter angle from Miter Table©

Outside corner LH piece

Fence

CCW

Outside corner Left-hand piece

http://www.compoundmiter.com, a Quint Group company, since March 2000

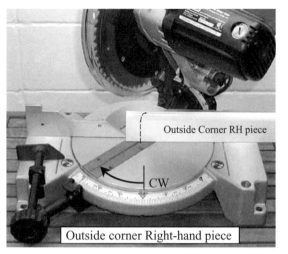

Outside corner Right-hand piece

Outside Corner Right-hand Piece

To cut the outside corner right-hand piece, rotate the miter setting on your saw clockwise to the same miter setting as in the 268° outside corner example above. You will then have the right-hand piece of the outside corner. To get a perfect joint every time, you should always measure the corner with an accurate angle-measuring tool. The True Angle® will provide the accuracy you need to obtain perfect joints.

Inside Corner Left-hand Piece

Using your True Angle®, measure the corner angle where you want to install the trim. Then obtain the miter angle setting you need from the Miter Table©. For the left-hand piece, rotate your miter saw clockwise to the miter angle for the corner you measured. Here I have set my miter for an inside corner cut for the left-hand piece. Let's say, as an example, you measured an inside corner of 93°. From the Miter Table© you get a miter setting of 43.5°. Set your saw on 43.5° as shown and make your cut.

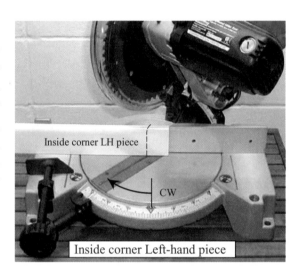

Inside corner Left-hand piece

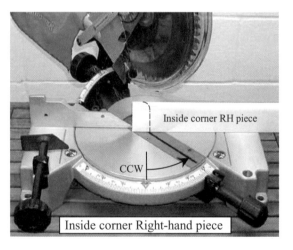

Inside corner Right-hand piece

Inside Corner Right-hand Piece

To cut the right-hand piece for an inside corner, rotate the miter setting on your saw counter-clockwise to the same miter setting as for the left-hand piece. You will then have the right-hand piece of the inside corner.

Upward/Downward Turns

Trim can also turn vertically when you are trimming a staircase or other areas that run at an incline or sloping angle. When you are making cuts for vertical turns using a miter saw, cut these exactly the same as when you are using a compound miter saw. See **Upward/Downward Turns** on page 21 for details on how to cut this type of turn using a miter saw.

Using a Compound Miter Saw
Horizontal Turns

If you have a compound miter saw, you can lay your trim flat on the saw table. I prefer using this method to cut all trim and crown molding simply because it is easier to hold, especially when cutting very small pieces. To cut the trim laying flat, all you need to do is set the blade tilt to the correct angle obtained from the Miter Table©. Use the same settings as in the examples above, except tilt the blade instead of rotating the miter table. The miter will remain set to 0°.

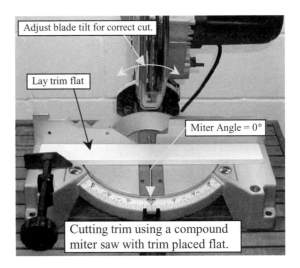

Cutting trim using a compound miter saw with trim placed flat.

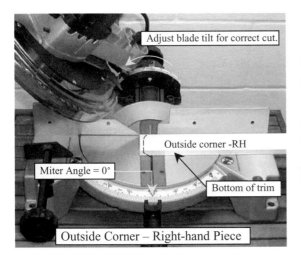

Outside Corner – Right-hand Piece

Outside Corner Right-hand Piece

Using the True Angle®, measure the corner angle where you would like to install the trim. To obtain the correct blade tilt, use the Miter Table© and read the angle which corresponds to the corner angle you measured. Place the trim flat on your saw with **the bottom of the trim towards you** and the blade tilted to the left to the correct angle.

Outside Corner Left-hand Piece

If you have already measured this corner angle in the previous step above and have not changed your saw settings, you are already set to cut the trim. Place the trim flat on your saw with the **top of the trim towards you** and the blade tilted to the left to the correct angle.

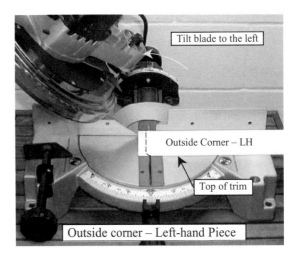

Outside corner – Left-hand Piece

Inside Corner Right-hand Piece

Using the True Angle®, measure the corner angle where you would like to install the trim. To obtain the correct blade tilt, go to the Miter Table© and read the angle that corresponds to the corner angle you measured. Place the trim flat on your saw with the **top towards you** and the blade set to the correct angle tilted to the left.

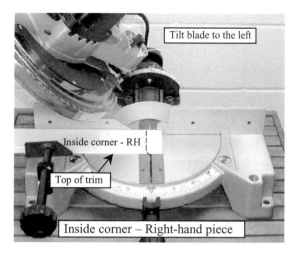

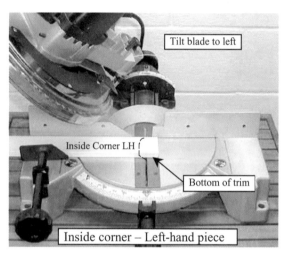

Inside Corner Left-hand Piece

If you have measured this corner angle in the previous step above and have not changed your saw settings, you are already set to cut the trim. Place the trim on your saw flat with the bottom of the trim towards you and the blade tilted to the left to the correct angle.

Templates

Inside Corners - Horizontal Turn

I strongly recommend you make a set of inside and outside corner templates for horizontal turns. Label them as shown in these two photos. Keep these with your miter saw and use them each time you get ready to cut a piece of trim. If you want to cut an inside corner right-hand piece, place that template on your saw and adjust the miter or blade tilt to match it.

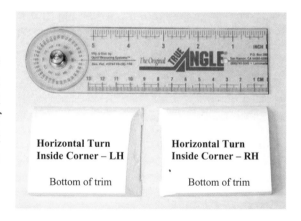

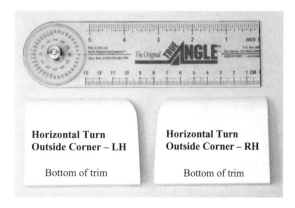

Outside Corners - Horizontal Turn

It does not matter what type saw you use (a miter saw, a compound miter saw, or a sliding compound miter saw), all left-hand and right-hand pieces for horizontal turns, inside and outside corners, will look just like these two templates.

Upward/Downward Turns (e.g., Stairs)

If you need to turn your trim up or down, you can cut your trim using a miter or a compound miter saw. With either saw, only use the miter adjustment and cut the trim placed flat and face-up on your saw. Simply measure the corner angle with your True Angle® and use the Miter Table© at the end of this chapter to get the miter setting.

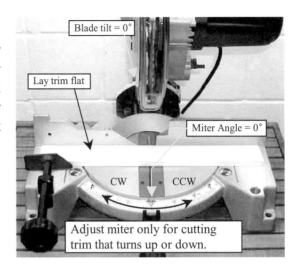

The next two pictures show how to set up your saw to cut trim if you want to turn upward. For the left-hand side, place the trim flat on the table with the top next to the fence, then set the miter counter-clockwise. For the right-hand side, do the same except rotate the miter clockwise. Measure the corner angle and get the correct miter angle from the Miter Table©.

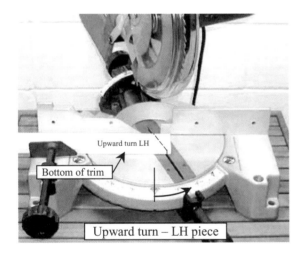

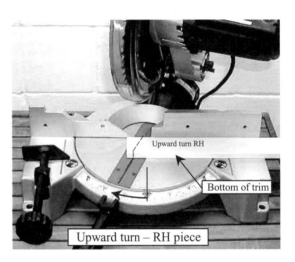

If you want to turn the trim downward, place the top of the trim next to the fence. For the left-hand side, rotate the miter clockwise. For the right-hand side, rotate the miter counter-clockwise.

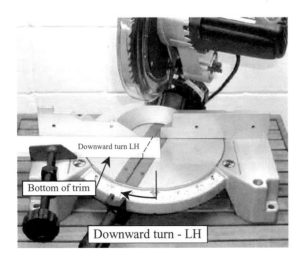

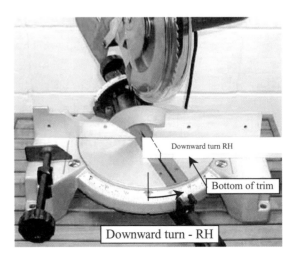

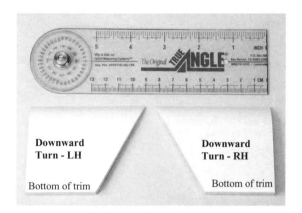

Downward Turn Templates

I highly recommend you make a set of downward and upward turn templates. Use the previous instructions, and label as shown in these two photos. Keep these with your miter saw and use them each time you get ready to cut a piece of trim. If you want to cut a downward turn left-hand piece, place that template on your saw and adjust the miter to the setting from the Miter Table©.

Upward Turn Templates

It does not matter what type of saw you use (a miter saw, a compound miter saw that tilts to the left or in both directions, or a sliding compound miter saw), all left-hand and right-hand pieces for upward/downward turns will look just like these templates. Only the miter/blade tilt will change depending on the corner angle the trim makes.

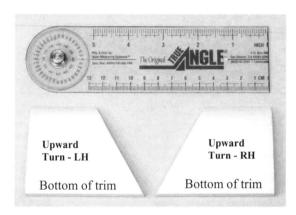

The Miter Table© is intended for use with a miter saw only. It will not work for making a compound miter cut. The Miter Table© will provide the angles needed for cutting trim that is installed flat on the surface. You can also install crown molding using the Miter Table©, but the crown will need to be propped up against the fence as described on page 24.

Summary and Review

Before you start cutting your trim, make a sketch of your work area using your True Angle® tool. Then measure each corner angle and each wall length. From this sketch, you can estimate the amount of trim needed to do the job (Chapter 1). You should also check to make sure your saw is square (Chapter 2). If your saw is out of square, every joint you cut will have a gap.

While cutting your trim using a miter saw or a compound miter saw, it is very important to **use your templates**. Your templates will prevent you from cutting your trim backward. Label them as shown and keep them with your saw. There is nothing more frustrating than cutting your trim and finding out that one end is cut backward. If the piece you cut backward isn't usable elsewhere, it becomes expensive firewood. To use your templates, find the template that matches the corner you need to cut. Place the template on your saw and position the miter and/or the blade tilt to match. Then set the miter and/or the blade tilt using the Miter Table© to make the perfect cut.

The Miter Table© will provide the miter angle needed for your saw. Just measure the corner angle with your True Angle®. Look up the corner angle in the Miter Table©, read the corresponding miter angle setting, and adjust your saw using the correct template as a guide.

The **Miter Table©** is used for cutting crown molding and trim with a miter saw. A compound miter saw can also be used if the blade tilt is set at 0° and only the miter angle is adjusted. Trim that is installed flat on the wall includes baseboards, chair rails, quarter and half round trim, cove molding, corner molding, fireplace trim, and door and window casings. You can also cut any crown molding using the Miter Table©, provided the crown molding is not too large for the saw being used. Visit our website at **www.compoundmiter.com** for the latest information on how to **Install Crown Molding and Trim Like a Pro!** (See instructions on page 24.)

Miter Table©

Corner Angle Inside or Outside	Miter Angle	Corner Angle Inside or Outside	Miter Angle	Corner Angle Inside or Outside	Miter Angle	Corner Angle Inside or Outside	Miter Angle
0 or 360	90.0	46 or 314	67.0	91 or 269	44.5	136 or 224	22.0
1 or 359	89.5	47 or 313	66.5	92 or 268	44.0	137 or 223	21.5
2 or 358	89.0	48 or 312	66.0	93 or 267	43.5	138 or 222	21.0
3 or 357	88.5	49 or 311	65.5	94 or 266	43.0	139 or 221	20.5
4 or 356	88.0	50 or 310	65.0	95 or 265	42.5	140 or 220	20.0
5 or 355	87.5	51 or 309	64.5	96 or 264	42.0	141 or 219	19.5
6 or 354	87.0	52 or 308	64.0	97 or 263	41.5	142 or 218	19.0
7 or 353	86.5	53 or 307	63.5	98 or 262	41.0	143 or 217	18.5
8 or 352	86.0	54 or 306	63.0	99 or 261	40.5	144 or 216	18.0
9 or 351	85.5	55 or 305	62.5	100 or 260	40.0	145 or 215	17.5
10 or 350	85.0	56 or 304	62.0	101 or 259	39.5	146 or 214	17.0
11 or 349	84.5	57 or 303	61.5	102 or 258	39.0	147 or 213	16.5
12 or 348	84.0	58 or 302	61.0	103 or 257	38.5	148 or 212	16.0
13 or 347	83.5	59 or 301	60.5	104 or 256	38.0	149 or 211	15.5
14 or 346	83.0	60 or 300	60.0	105 or 255	37.5	150 or 210	15.0
15 or 345	82.5	61 or 299	59.5	106 or 254	37.0	151 or 209	14.5
16 or 344	82.0	62 or 298	59.0	107 or 253	36.5	152 or 208	14.0
17 or 343	81.5	63 or 297	58.5	108 or 252	36.0	153 or 207	13.5
18 or 342	81.0	64 or 296	58.0	109 or 251	35.5	154 or 206	13.0
19 or 341	80.5	65 or 295	57.5	110 or 250	35.0	155 or 205	12.5
20 or 340	80.0	66 or 294	57.0	111 or 249	34.5	156 or 204	12.0
21 or 339	79.5	67 or 293	56.5	112 or 248	34.0	157 or 203	11.5
22 or 338	79.0	68 or 292	56.0	113 or 247	33.5	158 or 202	11.0
23 or 337	78.5	69 or 291	55.5	114 or 246	33.0	159 or 201	10.5
24 or 336	78.0	70 or 290	55.0	115 or 245	32.5	160 or 200	10.0
25 or 335	77.5	71 or 289	54.5	116 or 244	32.0	161 or 199	9.5
26 or 334	77.0	72 or 288	54.0	117 or 243	31.5	162 or 198	9.0
27 or 333	76.5	73 or 287	53.5	118 or 242	31.0	163 or 197	8.5
28 or 332	76.0	74 or 286	53.0	119 or 241	30.5	164 or 196	8.0
29 or 331	75.5	75 or 285	52.5	120 or 240	30.0	165 or 195	7.5
30 or 330	75.0	76 or 284	52.0	121 or 239	29.5	166 or 194	7.0
31 or 329	74.5	77 or 283	51.5	122 or 238	29.0	167 or 193	6.5
32 or 328	74.0	78 or 282	51.0	123 or 237	28.5	168 or 192	6.0
33 or 327	73.5	79 or 281	50.5	124 or 236	28.0	169 or 191	5.5
34 or 326	73.0	80 or 280	50.0	125 or 235	27.5	170 or 190	5.0
35 or 325	72.5	81 or 279	49.5	126 or 234	27.0	171 or 189	4.5
36 or 324	72.0	82 or 278	49.0	127 or 233	26.5	172 or 188	4.0
37 or 323	71.5	83 or 277	48.5	128 or 232	26.0	173 or 187	3.5
38 or 322	71.0	84 or 276	48.0	129 or 231	25.5	174 or 186	3.0
39 or 321	70.5	85 or 275	47.5	130 or 230	25.0	175 or 185	2.5
40 or 320	70.0	86 or 274	47.0	131 or 229	24.5	176 or 184	2.0
41 or 319	69.5	87 or 273	46.5	132 or 228	24.0	177 or 183	1.5
42 or 318	69.0	88 or 272	46.0	133 or 227	23.5	178 or 182	1.0
43 or 317	68.5	89 or 271	45.5	134 or 226	23.0	179 or 181	0.5
44 or 316	68.0	90 or 270	45.0	135 or 225	22.5	180 or 180	0.0
45 or 315	67.5	a Quint Group company		www.compoundmiter.com			

Instructions: Cutting Crown Molding and Trim Using a **Miter Saw**

Step 1. Using the True Angle® tool, measure the corner angle where you will be installing your crown molding or trim. (See drawing to the right.)

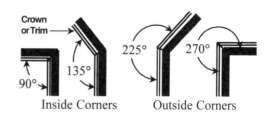

Step 2. Find the measured inside or outside corner angle in the Miter Table©. Read the miter angle in the adjacent column to the right.

Step 3. Locate the type of cut needed below. Rotate your miter table to the miter angle obtained in Step 2. Place the crown molding or trim on your miter saw to match the drawing. Make the perfect cut.

*Example: Crown molding, horizontal turn, inside corner at 135°, left-hand piece. **Answer:** Rotate the miter saw counter-clockwise to 22.5°. Position the crown to the right of the saw blade upside down with the bottom held firmly against the fence (see *Crown #4). Make the perfect cut.

Trim Installed Flat on the Wall

<u>Horizontal Turns</u>- Place trim standing up, bottom on miter table with the back against the fence.
Trim #1- Inside Corner/LH
Trim #2- Outside Corner/RH
Trim #3- Outside Corner/LH
Trim #4- Inside Corner/RH

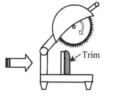

Side View (Miter Saw)

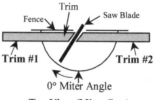

Top View (Miter Saw)

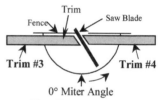

Top View (Miter Saw)

<u>Upward/Downward Turns</u>- (Cathedral ceilings, stairs, etc.) Lay trim face up, top against the fence.
Trim #5- Downward/LH
Trim #6- Upward/RH
Trim #7- Upward/LH
Trim #8- Downward/RH

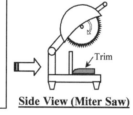

Side View (Miter Saw)

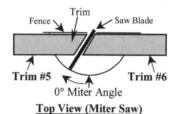

Top View (Miter Saw)

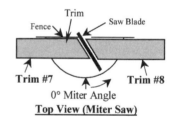

Top View (Miter Saw)

Crown Molding

<u>Horizontal Turns</u>
(Horizontal ceilings.) Hold bottom of crown against the fence.
Crown #1- Inside corner/RH
Crown #2- Outside corner/LH
Crown #3- Outside corner/RH
*Crown #4- Inside corner/LH

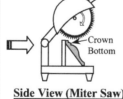

Side View (Miter Saw)

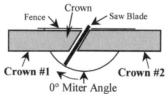

Top View (Miter Saw)

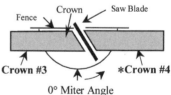

Top View (Miter Saw)

<u>Upward/Downward Turns</u> (Cathedral ceiling, stairs, etc.) Hold bottom of crown against the saw table.
Crown #5- Downward/LH
Crown #6- Upward/RH
Crown #7- Upward/LH
Crown #8- Downward/RH

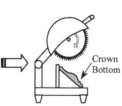

Side View (Miter Saw)

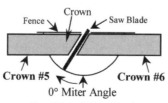

Top View (Miter Saw)

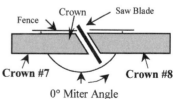

Top View (Miter Saw)

http://www.compoundmiter.com, a Quint Group company, since March 2000

Horizontal Ceilings

This chapter details the installation of crown molding on a horizontal ceiling. Use your True Angle® to measure the corner angle and either the Crown Molding Table© (for a compound miter saw) or the Miter Table© (for a miter saw) to get the correct angles needed to cut your crown. I will also cover the two types of corner turns for a horizontal ceiling, how to make your templates, laying out your work area, where to start, and how to install your crown.

First decide what size crown molding you want to install. The most common size used in a small-to-medium size bedroom is 3" to 4" crown. The larger crown moldings should be used in larger rooms. This, of course, is your choice. For this chapter, I will be installing 4" crown molding in a medium-size (15'x15') bedroom. (**Tip:** Paint your crown with two coats of paint before cutting and installing. When finished, you will only need to touch up your crown molding. This saves a lot of time.)

Inside and Outside Corners

Let's start by defining the basic cuts for a ***horizontal ceiling***. There are only two types, inside and outside corners. Inside corners are defined as any corner that measures between 0° and 180°. Outside corners are any corners that measure between 180° and 360°.

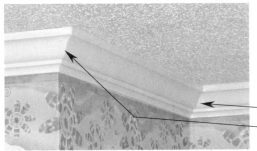

Here are examples of a 90° inside corner and a 270° outside corner. (These are cut somewhat differently, as I will demonstrate later.)

♦ Inside corners - corners that measure between 0° and 180°
♦ Outside corners - corners that measure between 180° and 360°

Laying Out the Work Area

Make a sketch of the room in which you will be installing the crown (Chapter 1). Use your True Angle® (18" minimum size) to measure all the corner angles, and a tape measure for the wall lengths. Place these on your sketch. It is very important that you measure as accurately as possible. We will later use the information from this sketch to cut the crown molding.

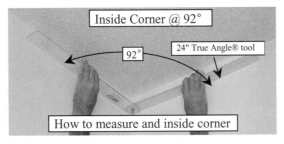

Inside Corner @ 92°

92° | 24" True Angle® tool

How to measure and inside corner

Here I am using my 24" True Angle® ***Crown Moulding Special*** to measure a 92° inside corner.

Note: Always measure the corner angle where the bottom of the crown will rest. If you measure the corner angle at eye level, the angle may not be the same where the crown will be placed. This applies to all trim.

This is an outside corner that measures 271°. The miter and blade tilt angles for this corner will be the same as for an inside corner that measures 89° (271°+89° = 360°). You will see both of the angle readings on the tool dial. The inner dial has the angles for an outside corner and the outer dial has the angles for an inside corner. Even though the miter and blade tilt angles are the same, we will stay with this descriptive difference because each is cut differently on your saw.

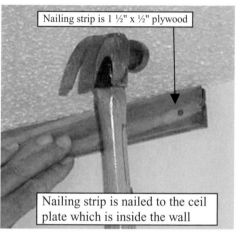

271°

24" Tool

Outside Corner @ 271°

Do I Need to Install Nailing Blocks/Strips?

If you are installing 3" crown, you will **not** need to install any blocks or strips. You should use 3" finishing nails. The larger the crown, the larger the nails will need to be. That is why blocks or strips are often installed first, then the crown nailed to those. Four inch crown can be installed with or without blocks or strips. If no blocks are used, 4" crown will require a minimum length nail of 3½". For this project, I will be installing 1½" x ½" plywood nailing strips and using 2½" finishing nails for the crown.

Nailing strip is 1 ½" x ½" plywood

Nailing strip is nailed to the ceil plate which is inside the wall

 [Blocks/Strips to nail crown to.]

To determine the size to cut the nailing blocks/strips, use a piece of crown to make a full-scale side view drawing of the corner (ceiling and wall). The blocks/strips should be no closer than 1/4" to the back of the crown. Just sketch whatever shape you want to cut in the hatched area of the drawing to the right, then use this to make your blocks/strips.

Before installing nailing blocks/strips, test drive a few nails into the wall around the perimeter of the ceiling behind where the crown will be installed. (A 2x4 usually runs horizontally inside the wall at the top.) If you do not hit wood at each place, use an electronic stud finder to locate the wall studs to nail the strips/blocks to.

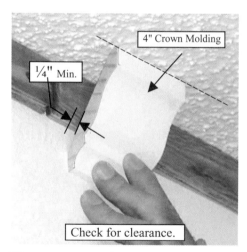

4" Crown Molding

¼" Min.

Check for clearance.

After you have installed the first nailing strip/block, make sure the crown does not touch the nailing strip. You should have a minimum of 1/4" of clearance. Once this is completed, continue all the way around the rest of the room with the nailing strip. Place one nail about every 2'.

Use your layout sketch to cut the nailing strips to length. Cut each piece at least 1" shorter than the wall length to avoid interference in the corners.

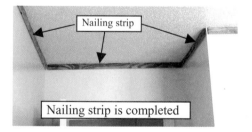

Nailing strip

Nailing strip is completed

We are now ready to start cutting and installing the crown molding. I have often been asked if texture on the ceiling should be removed. You do not need to remove it. Caulk will fill in the small voids. If your ceiling texture is very coarse and you would rather remove it than caulk, you can. Use a piece of your crown to mark where to remove the ceiling texture. (See photo above and to the left.)

Crown Angles

The two angles associated with crown molding are **spring angle** and **crown slope angle**.

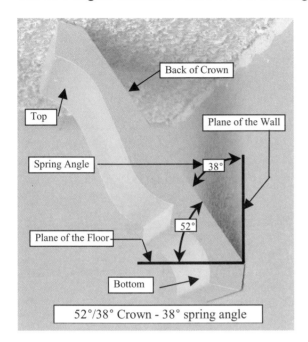

Top

Back of Crown

Plane of the Wall

Spring Angle — 38°

52°

Plane of the Floor

Bottom

52°/38° Crown - 38° spring angle

The **spring angle** is the angle measured from the back of the crown to the wall when installed. The crown molding in this example is 52°/38° crown. This is the most common type of crown molding. However, 45°/45° crown molding is also very common. **Be sure which type of crown you are using**. Check the spring angle of the crown with your True Angle® to make sure you do not wind up cutting 45°/45° crown molding as though you have 52°/38° crown molding. (To see how to measure the crown spring angle, go to page 34.) The crown molding found in most building supply stores may be improperly sorted. Customers hand-pick through the crown molding, often replacing it in the wrong stack. I have even purchased crown clearly marked 52° crown that turned out to be 45° crown. When purchasing crown, *always* take your 7" True Angle® and check the spring angle of each piece.

The **crown slope angle** is the angle from the back of the crown to the plane in which you are turning the crown. For example, horizontal turns of 52°/38° crown molding have a crown slope angle of 52°. (Use the 52° crown slope angle column in the Crown Molding Table©.) For horizontal turns using 45°/45° crown molding, the crown slope angle is 45°. (Use the 45° crown slope column in the Crown Molding Table©.)

Using a Miter Saw

This method of cutting crown is commonly referred to as **"Upside Down and Backwards"**. For this section, I will use a 10" compound miter saw that has blade tilt capability. I will set the blade tilt to 0° and use it as a miter saw. Only the miter setting will be adjusted. Set your miter saw as shown in the two pictures below to make your templates. When making your templates, use a corner angle of 90°/270° from the Miter Table© (Chapter 3) which shows a miter angle setting of 45°.

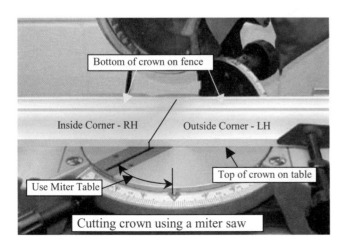

Bottom of crown on fence

Inside Corner - RH   Outside Corner - LH

Use Miter Table

Top of crown on table

Cutting crown using a miter saw

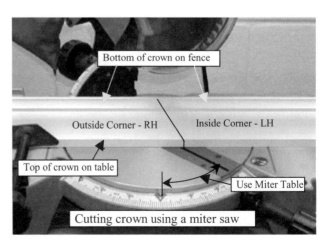

Bottom of crown on fence

Outside Corner - RH   Inside Corner - LH

Top of crown on table

Use Miter Table

Cutting crown using a miter saw

After you have cut the angles indicated in the above pictures, cut the templates about 3" long and label each one. You do not need to get confused trying to remember how to cut each piece. That is why the templates are so important. In the picture below, I am using templates to remind myself which way to place the crown in the saw and which direction to move the miter setting. Once you have decided how to place the crown on your saw, use your True Angle® to measure the corner angle or use the corner angle from the sketch made earlier. Set your miter angle obtained from the Miter Table© and make the cut. I would recommend first cutting your crown about 1/4" longer until you become familiar with how to measure and cut your crown. You can always trim more off later.

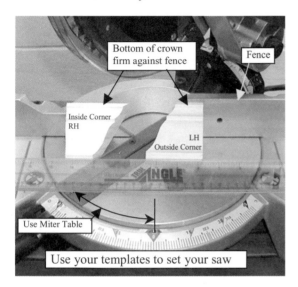

Use your templates to set your saw

It is important to remember to place the bottom of the crown firmly against the fence with the top of the crown resting on your saw table. Some crown molding manufacturers cut the angle of the top of the crown about 2° less, so you should not rely on the fit of the top against the table. If your fence is too short for the crown, extend the height by adding a board to your fence. Make sure the board is true and square (Chapter 2).

I cannot emphasize enough how important the templates are. Make yourself a set, or purchase a full set through our website. This will save you a lot of headaches and $$$.

Using a Compound Miter Saw

I will be using my 10" compound miter saw that only tilts to the left. This is the most common type. Some of the newer models tilt in both directions, making it easier to set and cut the crown. If your saw tilts in both directions, you will not need to rotate the crown. The final cuts will still look the same as your crown molding templates. To make templates using your compound miter saw, use 90° as the corner angle. From the Crown Molding Table©, included in this chapter, for a 52° crown slope angle (52°/38° crown making a horizontal turn), the miter angle is 31.6° and the blade tilt is 33.9°. If you are using 45°/45° crown, the crown slope angle for a horizontal turn is 45°.

Templates for Inside and Outside Corners

Inside Corner, Left-hand Template

This will be the piece of crown on your left while looking at an inside corner. Turn the compound miter saw table counter-clockwise to the correct miter setting. Tilt the saw to your left to the correct blade tilt angle. Use 90° as your corner angle to cut your templates. To obtain the miter and blade tilt angles from the Crown Molding Table©, use the 52° crown slope angle column (52°/38° crown turning horizontally). If you are using 45°/45° crown, use the 45° crown slope angle column. Place the top of the crown molding face up, flat on the table with the crown molding positioned to the left of the blade, and the top of the crown molding next to the fence. Make the cut.

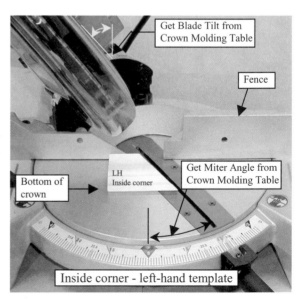

Inside corner - left-hand template

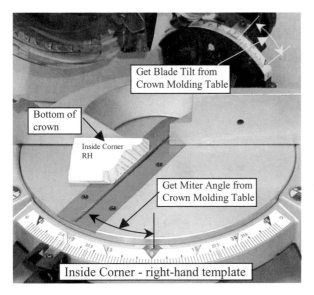

Get Blade Tilt from
Crown Molding Table

Bottom of
crown

Inside Corner
RH

Get Miter Angle from
Crown Molding Table

Inside Corner - right-hand template

Inside Corner, Right-hand Template

This will be the piece of crown on your right while looking at an inside corner, and this will also be the opposite mating crown for the template we just cut. Notice the changes I have made to the compound miter saw. The blade tilt position did not change. The miter table was rotated clockwise to the correct miter setting opposite the previous setting for the left-hand template.

I now have the bottom of the crown molding next to the compound miter saw fence, placed face up and flat on the table. Make the cut.

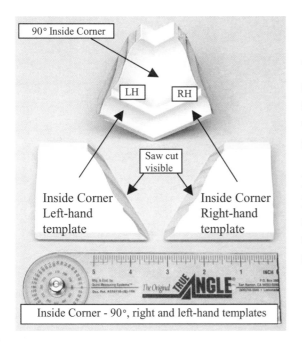

90° Inside Corner

LH   RH

Saw cut
visible

Inside Corner
Left-hand
template

Inside Corner
Right-hand
template

Inside Corner - 90°, right and left-hand templates

The right and left-hand inside corner templates I have just cut will *always* look like the photo to the left. Inside corners (left-hand and right-hand) will *always* have the saw cut visible and the pointed end will *always* be at the bottom of the crown molding.

Keep these templates with your saw. If you want to cut an inside corner, left-hand piece, place that template on your saw and adjust your saw in the correct direction to match the template. Using your templates will help prevent making the wrong cut.

Note: Always use the actual corner angle, not how much the corner turns. I occasionally receive an email saying, "I am cutting a 45° corner and none of the angles fit. What am I doing wrong?" In the example to the right, if you use 45° as the corner angle, you *will not* get the correct miter angle and blade tilt angle. **Use the angle the corner actually measures.** Here you would use 135° as the corner angle.

You now have your inside corner templates and all the information needed to cut inside corners for a horizontal plane.

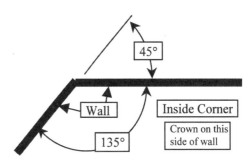

45°

Wall

Inside Corner

Crown on this
side of wall

135°

Outside Corner, Left-hand Template

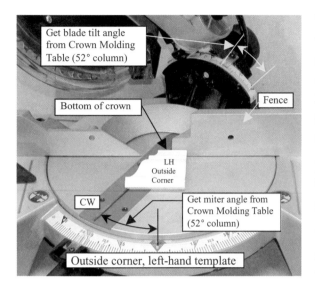

Get blade tilt angle from Crown Molding Table (52° column)

Bottom of crown

Fence

LH Outside Corner

CW

Get miter angle from Crown Molding Table (52° column)

Outside corner, left-hand template

To make an outside corner, left-hand template, I have turned my compound miter saw table clockwise to the correct miter setting and tilted the saw to the left to the correct blade tilt angle. For horizontal ceilings with 52°/38° crown, use the 52° crown slope angle column. If you are using 45°/45° crown, use the 45° crown slope angle column.

Place the crown molding face up, to the right of the saw blade, flat on the table, and with the bottom of the crown molding next to the fence. Make the cut.

You will not be able to see the saw-cut, and the pointed end will always be the top of the crown molding. This is the left-hand template for an outside corner.

Outside Corner, Right-hand Template

Notice the changes I have made to my compound miter saw. The blade tilt position did not change, but the miter table was rotated counter-clockwise to the correct miter setting opposite the previous setting for the left-hand template. I also now have the top of the crown molding (instead of the bottom) next to the compound miter saw fence, placed face up and flat on the table with the crown to the right of the saw blade.

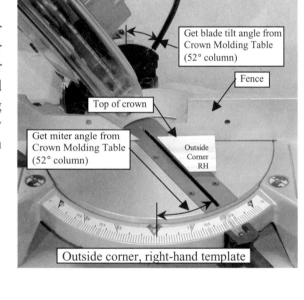

Get blade tilt angle from Crown Molding Table (52° column)

Fence

Top of crown

Get miter angle from Crown Molding Table (52° column)

Outside Corner RH

Outside corner, right-hand template

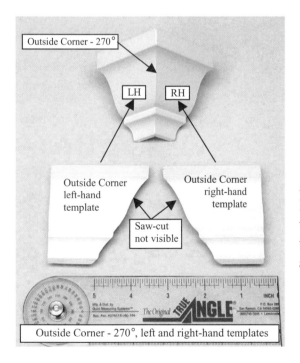

Outside Corner - 270°

LH   RH

Outside Corner left-hand template

Outside Corner right-hand template

Saw-cut not visible

Outside Corner - 270°, left and right-hand templates

All outside corner cuts for a horizontal ceiling will *always* look like these. When looking at the crown molding like it will be installed, the pointed ends will *always* be the top of the crown molding (next to the ceiling) and you will **not** be able to see the saw-cut surface.

How to Measure and Mark Crown Molding

Now that you have made your templates for horizontal turns and labeled them for inside and outside corners, it is time to cut and install your crown. Let's cover a little about how to place your wall length measurements on your crown and where to cut.

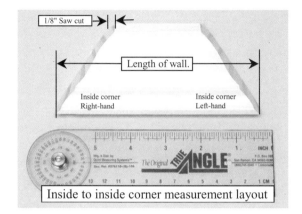

Inside to inside corner measurement layout

Inside Corner to Inside Corner: Measure the distance from the inside corner to the other inside corner of the wall. Layout the length of the wall on the bottom of your crown and cut the crown molding as shown. The measurement is from tip to tip on the crown (pointed end is at the bottom of the crown). If this is your first time, it is best to cut the crown about 1/4" too long, then trim to fit.

Inside Corner to Outside Corner: Measure the distance from the inside corner to the outside corner and cut the crown molding as shown. **Note:** When marking the crown on an outside corner, use the backside and bottom of the crown to place the length mark and cut to this. This is necessary because of the blade tilt angle. The backside of the crown molding (outside corner) must meet the corner of the wall.

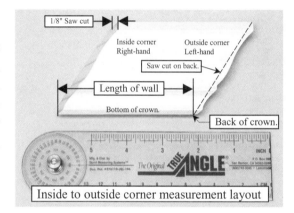

Inside to outside corner measurement layout

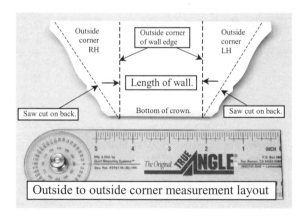

Outside to outside corner measurement layout

Outside Corner to Outside Corner: Measure the distance from outside corner to outside corner and cut the crown molding as shown. The length marks will be made on the bottom backside of the crown. **Note:** Again, when marking the crown on an outside corner, use the backside and bottom of the crown to place the length mark and cut to this. This is necessary because of the blade tilt angle. The backside of the crown molding (outside corner) must meet the corner of the wall. (Do not forget to take into account the 1/8" thickness of the saw blade on both sides and which side of your mark to make the cut.)

So far, you have made your templates, labeled them for inside and outside corners, and you understand how to transfer the wall length measurements from your sketch to your crown. It is time to start cutting and installing your crown. You should have already made a sketch of your work area as covered earlier. We will be using the dimensions and angles from the sketch to cut your crown.

Installing Your Crown Molding

Check your crown spring angle (page 34) so you will know the correct crown slope angle to use in the Crown Molding Table©. Start on the longest wall (Chapter 1) and cut the crown 1/4" longer than the dimension you have on your sketch. Then trim to fit. Use your templates as a guide to set your saw, using the miter and blade tilt angles for your corners and crown slope angle.

A word of caution: If you nail your crown too low or too high on the wall, you will have a gap in the joint at each corner. This is a common mistake, especially with larger crown molding. The best way to prevent this is to place a short piece of crown (6" to 12" long) with the bottom of the crown held firmly against the wall and slide it upward until it touches the ceiling. Draw a line at the bottom of the crown. Do this on both sides of your corners and at several locations along each wall. When installing your crown, you should then use this line as a guide for where to place the bottom of the crown (especially in the corners). Almost all ceilings have a little waviness, so your crown may dip below or above the marks along the wall, but the corners should match exactly.

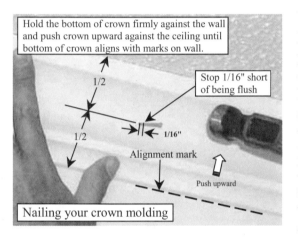

Hold the bottom of crown firmly against the wall and push crown upward against the ceiling until bottom of crown aligns with marks on wall.

1/2

Stop 1/16" short of being flush

1/2

1/16"

Alignment mark

Push upward

Nailing your crown molding

You are now ready to nail your first crown piece in place. Hold the crown firmly against the wall and slide it up into position until the alignment mark is at the bottom of your crown. This is where an extra set of hands comes in handy. Place the nail about midway to top and bottom of the crown and drive it in until the nail head is 1/16" from the surface of the crown molding. If you drive the nail flush, you will leave an indentation on the crown molding from your hammer that will show when you are finished. The nails should be spaced about 30" to 36" apart. To prevent splitting the crown, do not nail within 3" of the end without first drilling a nail hole.

If you are installing crown molding larger than the 4" crown shown here (5" and up), use two nails at each location. They should be spaced about 1/3 of the way from top and bottom. You will also need to use a nailing block or strip on which to nail the crown. For very large crown, it is recommended that nailing blocks be used, instead of a nailing strip, to save on wood. The blocks should be attached to every other wall stud (32" apart).

It is now time to set all of the nails. To do this, use a nail punch. Place the point of your punch in the small indentation on the top of the finishing nail. Hold firmly in place and square with the nail. This will prevent it from bouncing out of the small dimple in the nail head and making a hole in your crown. Tap your punch once lightly with your hammer. If the nail does not move, try again a little harder. Drive the nail, one tap at a time, until the nail is about 1/16" below the surface of the crown. ***Do not*** stop flush with the crown surface. If you stop flush, the touch-up paint over the nail head will probably flake off with time. Also, the spackling

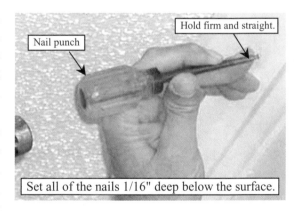

Nail punch

Hold firm and straight.

Set all of the nails 1/16" deep below the surface.

will not cover the nail head very well. Congratulations! You have just installed your first piece of crown.

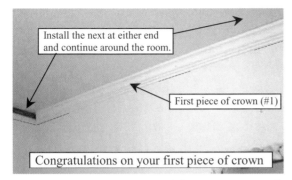

Install the next at either end and continue around the room.

First piece of crown (#1)

Congratulations on your first piece of crown

Continue around the rest of the room installing the remainder of your crown either in a clockwise or counter-clockwise direction.

Be sure to measure each corner angle with your True Angle®, or use the corner angle from the sketch you made earlier, to get the correct miter and blade tilt angles to cut each piece of crown.

Use your templates to position your saw when you cut any piece of crown. Rotate the miter table and tilt the saw blade to match the template, and set the saw miter and blade tilt angles you obtained from the Crown Molding Table© or Miter Excel Program©. (If you are using a miter saw, use the Miter Table© in Chapter 3 to get the settings for your saw.) Remember to allow about 1/4" extra length until you become experienced at cutting crown.

You should now have all of your crown molding installed and all nails correctly countersunk about 1/16" deep. You are now ready to caulk your crown molding/trim (Chapter 9).

Summary and Review

You now have all the basics on how to cut and install crown molding for a room with a horizontal ceiling. After you make your templates as shown in this chapter, you will be able to reference these while cutting the crown and avoid those costly and frustrating mistakes of cutting the crown backward.

Remember, the corners in your house that look 90° can be out of square as much as 3° (Chapter 1). That is why it is so important to measure the corner angle with The Original True Angle® tool, then use the Crown Molding Table© or the Miter Excel Program© to get the exact miter and blade tilt angles needed. (Use the Miter Table© if using a miter saw.)

Here are a few **very important** things to remember when installing your crown:
1. Always **use your True Angle®** to measure your corners.
2. Always **check your crown spring angle** (angle from the wall to the back of the crown). If you are installing crown with a 45° spring angle, and you cut it using the angles for 38° spring angle crown, *your corners will not fit*.
3. Always **use your templates** for each cut to ensure the correct placement of the crown and which direction to rotate the saw blade.
4. Always **place alignment marks on the wall** at the bottom of the crown. To do this, take a 6" to 12" piece of crown and place the bottom firmly on the wall and slide it up until it just touches the ceiling. Draw a short line on the wall at the bottom of the crown and use this mark to position your crown when installing. Mark each side of each corner and then 2 or 3 places along each wall. You should make every effort to place your crown exactly on the corner alignment marks.

The Crown Molding Table© has all the miter and blade tilt angles needed to install crown molding on a horizontal ceiling for both 38° and 45° spring angle crown.

How long should the nails be? You should have at least 1" of nail driven into the wood in the wall. This 1" does not include the dry-wall thickness. Nail into the 2x4 which runs horizontally inside the wall at the top. If you cannot find this 2x4, nail into the wall studs. Blocks or nailing strips are needed when installing large crown molding (5+ inches).

What are the most common crown spring angles? The two most common spring angles are 38° (52°/38°crown) and 45° (45°/45° crown). The first number is the angle the back of the crown makes with a horizontal plane (the floor). The second number is the angle the back of the crown makes with a vertical plane (the wall), also known as the spring angle of the crown. The crown I have used for this chapter is a 52°/38° crown. For **all** horizontal crown turns, use the first number as the crown slope angle in all of the compound miter tables/charts/program. The second number will be the crown slope angle for installing crown that makes upward/downward turns (e.g., cathedral/vaulted ceilings).

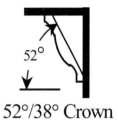

52°/38° Crown

How to Measure Your Crown Spring Angle

There are crowns manufactured with spring angles other than 38° and 45°. Always check to see which one you have before making any cuts.

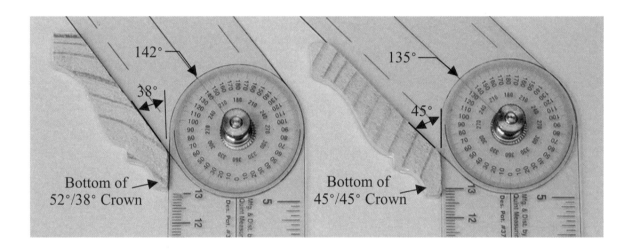

Note: **Extremely important**. Take a close look at the two crowns in the above picture. Do you see any difference between them? The one on the left is 52°/38° crown (spring angle = 38°); the one on the right is 45°/45° crown (spring angle = 45°). Cutting 45°/45° crown, thinking you have 52°/38° crown, will leave gaps in the joints. Measure the spring angle of your crown molding **before you cut**.

To check the crown spring angle, set your True Angle® on 142° and hold it on the crown molding as in the photo above. If the tool fits the bottom of the crown molding while set at 142°, you have 52°/38° crown. If it does not fit, set your tool on 135° and try again. If it fits while set at 135°, you have 45°/45° crown. If your crown measures something different, you have a nonstandard crown. To get the spring angle for the nonstandard crown, subtract the angle you measured with the True Angle® from 180°. For example, if your crown measures 150° (180°-150° = 30°), you have 30° spring angle crown (60°/30° crown molding). You would then use the Compound Miter Chart© to get the miter and blade tilt angles.

INSTRUCTIONS: This table is for use with a <u>compound miter saw</u>, crown placed flat and face up. For a <u>miter saw</u>, you will need the **Miter Table©**. The **Crown Slope Angle** is the angle between the back of the crown (when installed) and the plane in which you are turning the crown. Example: For 52°/38° crown turning in a horizontal plane (standard horizontal ceiling), the crown slope angle is 52°. For 52°/38° crown turning in a vertical plane (cathedral ceiling application), the crown slope angle is 38°. For 45°/45° crown, the crown slope angle is 45° (horizontal or vertical turns).

52°/38° Crown

Crown Molding Table©

Corner Angle (Inside or Outside)	Crown Slope Angle 52° Miter Angle	52° Blade Tilt	45° Miter Angle	45° Blade Tilt	38° Miter Angle	38° Blade Tilt	Corner Angle (Inside or Outside)	Crown Slope Angle 52° Miter Angle	52° Blade Tilt	45° Miter Angle	45° Blade Tilt	38° Miter Angle	38° Blade Tilt
0 or 360	90.0	52.0	90.0	45.0	90.0	38.0	46 or 314	55.4	46.5	59.0	40.6	61.7	34.5
1 or 359	89.2	52.0	89.3	45.0	89.4	38.0	47 or 313	54.8	46.3	58.4	40.4	61.1	34.4
2 or 358	88.4	52.0	88.6	45.0	88.7	38.0	48 or 312	54.1	46.0	57.8	40.2	60.5	34.2
3 or 357	87.6	52.0	87.9	45.0	88.1	38.0	49 or 311	53.5	45.8	57.2	40.0	60.0	34.1
4 or 356	86.8	52.0	87.2	45.0	87.5	38.0	50 or 310	52.9	45.6	56.6	39.9	59.4	33.9
5 or 355	85.9	51.9	86.5	44.9	86.8	38.0	51 or 309	52.2	45.3	56.0	39.7	58.8	33.8
6 or 354	85.1	51.9	85.8	44.9	86.2	37.9	52 or 308	51.6	45.1	55.4	39.5	58.2	33.6
7 or 353	84.3	51.9	85.1	44.9	85.6	37.9	53 or 307	51.0	44.8	54.8	39.3	57.7	33.4
8 or 352	83.5	51.8	84.4	44.9	84.9	37.9	54 or 306	50.4	44.6	54.2	39.1	57.1	33.3
9 or 351	82.7	51.8	83.6	44.8	84.3	37.9	55 or 305	49.8	44.3	53.6	38.8	56.6	33.1
10 or 350	81.9	51.7	82.9	44.8	83.7	37.8	56 or 304	49.2	44.1	53.1	38.6	56.0	32.9
11 or 349	81.1	51.7	82.2	44.7	83.0	37.8	57 or 303	48.6	43.8	52.5	38.4	55.4	32.8
12 or 348	80.3	51.6	81.5	44.7	82.4	37.8	58 or 302	48.0	43.6	51.9	38.2	54.9	32.6
13 or 347	79.5	51.5	80.8	44.6	81.8	37.7	59 or 301	47.4	43.3	51.3	38.0	54.3	32.4
14 or 346	78.7	51.5	80.1	44.6	81.1	37.7	60 or 300	46.8	43.0	50.8	37.8	53.8	32.2
15 or 345	77.9	51.4	79.5	44.5	80.5	37.6	61 or 299	46.3	42.8	50.2	37.5	53.2	32.0
16 or 344	77.1	51.3	78.8	44.4	79.9	37.6	62 or 298	45.7	42.5	49.6	37.3	52.7	31.9
17 or 343	76.4	51.2	78.1	44.4	79.3	37.5	63 or 297	45.1	42.2	49.1	37.1	52.1	31.7
18 or 342	75.6	51.1	77.4	44.3	78.6	37.5	64 or 296	44.6	41.9	48.5	36.8	51.6	31.5
19 or 341	74.8	51.0	76.7	44.2	78.0	37.4	65 or 295	44.0	41.7	48.0	36.6	51.0	31.3
20 or 340	74.0	50.9	76.0	44.1	77.4	37.3	66 or 294	43.5	41.4	47.4	36.4	50.5	31.1
21 or 339	73.2	50.8	75.3	44.0	76.8	37.3	67 or 293	42.9	41.1	46.9	36.1	50.0	30.9
22 or 338	72.5	50.7	74.6	44.0	76.1	37.2	68 or 292	42.4	40.8	46.4	35.9	49.4	30.7
23 or 337	71.7	50.6	73.9	43.9	75.5	37.1	69 or 291	41.9	40.5	45.8	35.6	48.9	30.5
24 or 336	71.0	50.4	73.3	43.8	74.9	37.0	70 or 290	41.3	40.2	45.3	35.4	48.4	30.3
25 or 335	70.2	50.3	72.6	43.7	74.3	36.9	71 or 289	40.8	39.9	44.8	35.1	47.8	30.1
26 or 334	69.4	50.2	71.9	43.5	73.7	36.9	72 or 288	40.3	39.6	44.2	34.9	47.3	29.9
27 or 333	68.7	50.0	71.2	43.4	73.1	36.8	73 or 287	39.8	39.3	43.7	34.6	46.8	29.7
28 or 332	68.0	49.9	70.6	43.3	72.4	36.7	74 or 286	39.2	39.0	43.2	34.4	46.3	29.5
29 or 331	67.2	49.7	69.9	43.2	71.8	36.6	75 or 285	38.7	38.7	42.7	34.1	45.8	29.2
30 or 330	66.5	49.6	69.2	43.1	71.2	36.5	76 or 284	38.2	38.4	42.1	33.9	45.2	29.0
31 or 329	65.8	49.4	68.6	43.0	70.6	36.4	77 or 283	37.7	38.1	41.6	33.6	44.7	28.8
32 or 328	65.0	49.2	67.9	42.8	70.0	36.3	78 or 282	37.2	37.8	41.1	33.3	44.2	28.6
33 or 327	64.3	49.1	67.3	42.7	69.4	36.2	79 or 281	36.8	37.4	40.6	33.1	43.7	28.4
34 or 326	63.6	48.9	66.6	42.5	68.8	36.1	80 or 280	36.3	37.1	40.1	32.8	43.2	28.1
35 or 325	62.9	48.7	66.0	42.4	68.2	36.0	81 or 279	35.8	36.8	39.6	32.5	42.7	27.9
36 or 324	62.2	48.5	65.3	42.3	67.6	35.8	82 or 278	35.3	36.5	39.1	32.3	42.2	27.7
37 or 323	61.5	48.4	64.7	42.1	67.0	35.7	83 or 277	34.8	36.2	38.6	32.0	41.7	27.5
38 or 322	60.8	48.2	64.0	42.0	66.4	35.6	84 or 276	34.4	35.8	38.1	31.7	41.2	27.2
39 or 321	60.1	48.0	63.4	41.8	65.8	35.5	85 or 275	33.9	35.5	37.7	31.4	40.7	27.0
40 or 320	59.4	47.8	62.8	41.6	65.2	35.3	86 or 274	33.4	35.2	37.2	31.1	40.2	26.8
41 or 319	58.7	47.6	62.1	41.5	64.6	35.2	87 or 273	33.0	34.9	36.7	30.9	39.7	26.5
42 or 318	58.1	47.4	61.5	41.3	64.0	35.1	88 or 272	32.5	34.5	36.2	30.6	39.2	26.3
43 or 317	57.4	47.2	60.9	41.1	63.4	34.9	89 or 271	32.1	34.2	35.7	30.3	38.7	26.0
44 or 316	56.7	46.9	60.3	41.0	62.9	34.8	90 or 270	31.6	33.9	35.3	30.0	38.2	25.8
45 or 315	56.1	46.7	59.6	40.8	62.3	34.7	www.compoundmiter.com						

The **Corner Angle** is the measured angle of the corner. Use your True Angle® tool to measure the true corner angle formed by the crown molding. Find your measured corner angle in the Crown Molding Table© and read across to the right to get the miter and blade tilt angles for the crown slope angle you have. (0° miter is a square cut, 0° blade tilt is a vertical blade). For all of the latest, visit us @ **http://www.compoundmiter.com,** a Quint Group company.

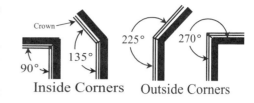

Inside Corners   Outside Corners

Crown Molding Table©

Corner Angle	Crown Slope Angle						Corner Angle	Crown Slope Angle					
	52°		45°		38°			52°		45°		38°	
Inside or Outside	Miter Angle	Blade Tilt	Miter Angle	Blade Tilt	Miter Angle	Blade Tilt	Inside or Outside	Miter Angle	Blade Tilt	Miter Angle	Blade Tilt	Miter Angle	Blade Tilt
91 or 269	31.2	33.5	34.8	29.7	37.8	25.6	136 or 224	14.0	17.2	15.9	15.4	17.7	13.3
92 or 268	30.7	33.2	34.3	29.4	37.3	25.3	137 or 223	13.6	16.8	15.6	15.0	17.2	13.0
93 or 267	30.3	32.8	33.9	29.1	36.8	25.1	138 or 222	13.3	16.4	15.2	14.7	16.8	12.7
94 or 266	29.9	32.5	33.4	28.8	36.3	24.8	139 or 221	13.0	16.0	14.8	14.3	16.4	12.5
95 or 265	29.4	32.2	32.9	28.5	35.8	24.6	140 or 220	12.6	15.6	14.4	14.0	16.0	12.2
96 or 264	29.0	31.8	32.5	28.2	35.4	24.3	141 or 219	12.3	15.3	14.1	13.7	15.6	11.9
97 or 263	28.6	31.5	32.0	27.9	34.9	24.1	142 or 218	12.0	14.9	13.7	13.3	15.2	11.6
98 or 262	28.2	31.1	31.6	27.6	34.4	23.8	143 or 217	11.6	14.5	13.3	13.0	14.8	11.3
99 or 261	27.7	30.8	31.1	27.3	33.9	23.6	144 or 216	11.3	14.1	12.9	12.6	14.4	11.0
100 or 260	27.3	30.4	30.7	27.0	33.5	23.3	145 or 215	11.0	13.7	12.6	12.3	14.0	10.7
101 or 259	26.9	30.1	30.2	26.7	33.0	23.1	146 or 214	10.7	13.3	12.2	11.9	13.5	10.4
102 or 258	26.5	29.7	29.8	26.4	32.5	22.8	147 or 213	10.3	12.9	11.8	11.6	13.1	10.1
103 or 257	26.1	29.4	29.4	26.1	32.1	22.5	148 or 212	10.0	12.5	11.5	11.2	12.7	9.8
104 or 256	25.7	29.0	28.9	25.8	31.6	22.3	149 or 211	9.7	12.2	11.1	10.9	12.3	9.5
105 or 255	25.3	28.7	28.5	25.5	31.2	22.0	150 or 210	9.4	11.8	10.7	10.5	11.9	9.2
106 or 254	24.9	28.3	28.1	25.2	30.7	21.7	151 or 209	9.0	11.4	10.4	10.2	11.5	8.9
107 or 253	24.5	28.0	27.6	24.9	30.2	21.5	152 or 208	8.7	11.0	10.0	9.8	11.1	8.6
108 or 252	24.1	27.6	27.2	24.6	29.8	21.2	153 or 207	8.4	10.6	9.6	9.5	10.7	8.3
109 or 251	23.7	27.2	26.8	24.2	29.3	20.9	154 or 206	8.1	10.2	9.3	9.2	10.3	8.0
110 or 250	23.3	26.9	26.3	23.9	28.9	20.7	155 or 205	7.8	9.8	8.9	8.8	9.9	7.7
111 or 249	22.9	26.5	25.9	23.6	28.4	20.4	156 or 204	7.5	9.4	8.5	8.5	9.5	7.4
112 or 248	22.6	26.1	25.5	23.3	28.0	20.1	157 or 203	7.1	9.0	8.2	8.1	9.1	7.1
113 or 247	22.2	25.8	25.1	23.0	27.5	19.9	158 or 202	6.8	8.6	7.8	7.8	8.7	6.7
114 or 246	21.8	25.4	24.7	22.7	27.1	19.6	159 or 201	6.5	8.3	7.5	7.4	8.3	6.4
115 or 245	21.4	25.0	24.3	22.3	26.7	19.3	160 or 200	6.2	7.9	7.1	7.1	7.9	6.1
116 or 244	21.0	24.7	23.8	22.0	26.2	19.0	161 or 199	5.9	7.5	6.7	6.7	7.5	5.8
117 or 243	20.7	24.3	23.4	21.7	25.8	18.8	162 or 198	5.6	7.1	6.4	6.4	7.1	5.5
118 or 242	20.3	23.9	23.0	21.4	25.3	18.5	163 or 197	5.3	6.7	6.0	6.0	6.7	5.2
119 or 241	19.9	23.6	22.6	21.0	24.9	18.2	164 or 196	4.9	6.3	5.7	5.6	6.3	4.9
120 or 240	19.6	23.2	22.2	20.7	24.5	17.9	165 or 195	4.6	5.9	5.3	5.3	5.9	4.6
121 or 239	19.2	22.8	21.8	20.4	24.0	17.6	166 or 194	4.3	5.5	5.0	4.9	5.5	4.3
122 or 238	18.8	22.5	21.4	20.0	23.6	17.4	167 or 193	4.0	5.1	4.6	4.6	5.1	4.0
123 or 237	18.5	22.1	21.0	19.7	23.2	17.1	168 or 192	3.7	4.7	4.3	4.2	4.7	3.7
124 or 236	18.1	21.7	20.6	19.4	22.7	16.8	169 or 191	3.4	4.3	3.9	3.9	4.3	3.4
125 or 235	17.8	21.3	20.2	19.1	22.3	16.5	170 or 190	3.1	3.9	3.5	3.5	3.9	3.1
126 or 234	17.4	21.0	19.8	18.7	21.9	16.2	171 or 189	2.8	3.5	3.2	3.2	3.5	2.8
127 or 233	17.1	20.6	19.4	18.4	21.4	15.9	172 or 188	2.5	3.2	2.8	2.8	3.2	2.5
128 or 232	16.7	20.2	19.0	18.1	21.0	15.7	173 or 187	2.2	2.8	2.5	2.5	2.8	2.2
129 or 231	16.4	19.8	18.6	17.7	20.6	15.4	174 or 186	1.8	2.4	2.1	2.1	2.4	1.8
130 or 230	16.0	19.5	18.2	17.4	20.2	15.1	175 or 185	1.5	2.0	1.8	1.8	2.0	1.5
131 or 229	15.7	19.1	17.9	17.1	19.8	14.8	176 or 184	1.2	1.6	1.4	1.4	1.6	1.2
132 or 228	15.3	18.7	17.5	16.7	19.3	14.5	177 or 183	0.9	1.2	1.1	1.1	1.2	0.9
133 or 227	15.0	18.3	17.1	16.4	18.9	14.2	178 or 182	0.6	0.8	0.7	0.7	0.8	0.6
134 or 226	14.6	17.9	16.7	16.0	18.5	13.9	179 or 181	0.3	0.4	0.4	0.4	0.4	0.3
135 or 225	14.3	17.6	16.3	15.7	18.1	13.6	180 or 180	0.0	0.0	0.0	0.0	0.0	0.0
Quint Measuring Systems, Inc.							www.compoundmiter.com						

Cathedral/Vaulted Ceilings

In this chapter, we will be installing crown molding on a cathedral ceiling. You will need your True Angle® tool, the Crown Molding Table© (Chapter 4), and possibly the Compound Miter Chart© (this chapter) or the Miter Excel Program©. The minimum size True Angle® tool we recommend is the 18" tool. If you have walls shorter than 18", you will also need the shorter tools found in the "Best Value True Angle® Tool Package" which contains the 7", 12", 18" and 23" tools. All of these products can be purchased through our website.

If you have not read and understood Chapter 4 on how to install crown molding on a horizontal ceiling, you need to stop and do so. You must understand how to:
1. Measure inside and outside corner angles using your True Angle®.
2. Use the Miter Table©, Crown Molding Table© or the Miter Excel Program©.
3. Make your templates for inside and outside corners for a horizontal ceiling.
4. Measure/mark/cut your crown molding for inside and outside corners.
5. Position your crown on the wall using alignment marks.

Now that you know how to cut and install crown molding on a horizontal ceiling, let's proceed with your rooms that have cathedral/vaulted ceilings. Cathedral ceilings are sometimes very confusing, but if you follow me through this section and understand the basics, you will be able to quickly master the cathedral/vaulted ceiling.

Turning Your Crown in the Ceiling Plane
(This is very important.)
There are three planes in which you can make turns with your crown. A plane is nothing more than a flat surface. For example, when you install crown in a room with a horizontal ceiling and come to a corner, you are making a turn of the crown in a **horizontal plane**. Every corner turn made in Chapter 4 was in a **horizontal plane**. (Joint "A" below is a turn in the horizontal plane.) I will introduce to you two other planes in which you can turn crown molding.

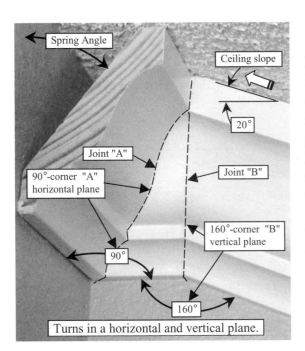

Turns in a horizontal and vertical plane.

Let's discuss the **vertical plane** (the plane of the wall). This is done when you are turning the crown upwards or downwards as shown at joint "B". The corner at joint "B" is an inside 160° (180° - 20° = 160°) corner in the **vertical plane**. The example to the left is where the crown is running horizontally (left to right), then makes a 90° turn in the corner (horizontal plane) and must turn downward (vertical plane) to follow the 20° sloping ceiling.

The **ceiling plane** (the plane of the ceiling) is the third one which we will cover later in this chapter.

Crown Angles for Cathedral/Vaulted Ceilings

Crown Slope Angle

So far, we have discussed the three planes in which you can turn crown molding. Now we need to define and explain the crown slope angle again. (Chapter 4 only dealt with the crown slope angle in the horizontal plane.) The **crown slope angle** is defined as the angle between the back of the crown and the plane in which the corner is making a turn. In other words, it is the angle from the back of the crown molding to the **horizontal plane**, the **vertical plane**, or the **ceiling plane**. Whichever plane you are turning the crown molding in, that corner will determine the crown slope angle to use in the compound miter charts/tables/program. Take a look at this photo and memorize the three crown slope angles.

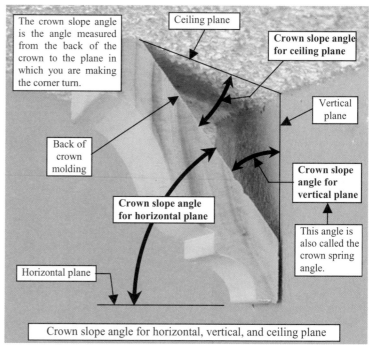

The crown slope angle is the angle measured from the back of the crown to the plane in which you are making the corner turn.

Ceiling plane

Crown slope angle for ceiling plane

Vertical plane

Back of crown molding

Crown slope angle for vertical plane

This angle is also called the crown spring angle.

Crown slope angle for horizontal plane

Horizontal plane

Crown slope angle for horizontal, vertical, and ceiling plane

Crown Spring Angle

The **crown spring angle** is the angle measured from the back of the crown to the wall. Also notice the **crown slope angle** is the same as the **crown spring angle** when turning the crown in a vertical plane. If you purchase 38° spring angle crown, that crown molding will make a 38° angle between the back of the crown and the wall. If you purchase 45° spring angle crown, the angle from the back of the crown to the wall will be 45°. These two crown molding spring angles are the most common. However, there are some crowns manufactured with different spring angles. Always use your True Angle® tool to measure the crown spring angle (see page 34). The Compound Miter Chart© will provide the miter and blade tilt angles for nonstandard crown molding. Spend some time reviewing the above information. It is very important that you understand the difference between crown spring angle and crown slope angle.

For the remainder of the chapter, I will provide examples of some common cathedral/vaulted ceiling corners. The **corner angle** and the **crown slope angle** are all the information you need to get the correct miter and blade tilt angles from our compound miter products. Now let's make our set of templates for crown molding turning in a vertical plane.

Cathedral/Vaulted Ceiling Templates

Corner Templates for a Vertical Plane

You have already made both sets of templates (inside and outside corners for a horizontal/ceiling plane) as covered in Chapter 4. You will need both sets, plus you will need to make another set of templates for inside and outside corners when turning the crown in a vertical plane (plane of the wall). The horizontal plane templates can also be used for crown molding turns in the ceiling plane. They are identical so you will not need to make a set for the ceiling plane.

Outside Corner Templates for Vertical Plane

The most common cathedral ceiling corner is where the crown is running along a horizontal wall (left to right), reaching a 90° corner, then turning upward to continue along the cathedral ceiling. Notice the small wedge-shaped crown piece #2 between #1 and #3. Piece #2 is necessary so you will **not** change the spring angle of the crown. I will address this later in this chapter but for now, let's just get your templates made for a vertical plane. This set of templates will be for joint "B", outside corner in a vertical plane.

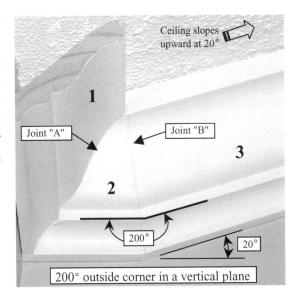
200° outside corner in a vertical plane

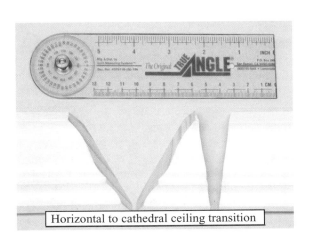
Horizontal to cathedral ceiling transition

This is what the crown molding will look like when it is cut and ready to install for a horizontal to cathedral ceiling transition. Notice joint "A" is made by using your inside corner templates for a horizontal plane. Let's make our templates for the outside corner, vertical plane (joint "B").

Left-hand Outside Corner Template, Vertical Plane

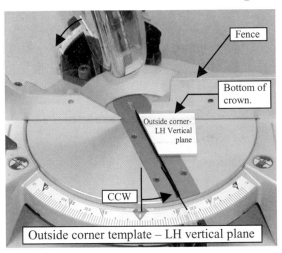
Outside corner template – LH vertical plane

To make your left-hand template for an outside corner turn in a vertical plane, place the crown face up with the bottom of the crown against the fence. Tilt the blade to the left and rotate the miter counter-clockwise. Your crown will be positioned to the right of the saw blade.

The **crown slope angle** for joint "B" (above) is 38° (same as the spring angle, page 38). In our example, the corner angle is 200° and the crown slope angle is 38°. From the Crown Molding Table©, you can see the miter angle would be 7.9° and the blade tilt is 6.1°. Let's use 225° as the corner angle (instead of 200°) to make your templates. From the Crown Molding Table©, using a corner angle of 225° and a crown slope angle of 38°, the miter angle is 18.1° and the blade tilt angle is 13.6°.

For your left-hand outside corner template, vertical plane, rotate your miter table counter-clockwise to 18.1° and tilt your blade to the left to 13.6°. Place your crown (bottom against the fence) to the right of the blade and make the cut.

Right-hand Outside Corner Template, Vertical Plane

Now let's cut your template for the right-hand side of an outside corner turning in a vertical plane. Place your crown on your saw, face up, with the top of the crown against the fence. Rotate the miter table clockwise to the correct miter setting and the blade tilt to the left to the correct setting. Again, these settings are obtained from the Crown Molding Table© on page 36, using a corner angle of 225° and a crown slope angle of 38°. Remember, for these examples we are using crown molding that has a spring angle of 38°. If you have crown molding with a spring angle of 45°, you would use the 45° column in the Crown Molding Table©.

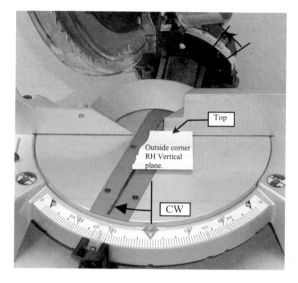

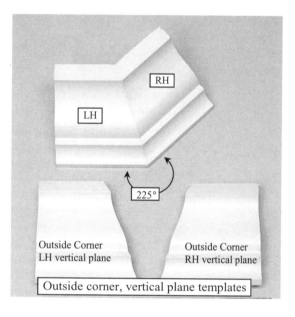

You now have completed your set of outside corner templates for turns in a vertical plane to add to your collection. Cut the templates about 3" long and label as shown.

Inside Corner Templates for Vertical Plane

Joint "B" to the right is an example of an inside corner turn in a vertical plane. Inside corners are corners that are less than 180°. In this example, we have a 20° sloping ceiling which will make a 160° inside corner when turning the crown as shown. This cathedral corner is opposite the cathedral corner we just looked at (above) where the crown made an outside corner turn in the vertical plane (turning upward). Here the crown is running horizontally (left to right) and needs to make a turn downward to follow the cathedral ceiling. Again, we will need to cut a small wedge piece to make this transition. This wedge piece is needed so that we will **not** change the spring angle of the crown. We are now ready to make the last set of templates needed.

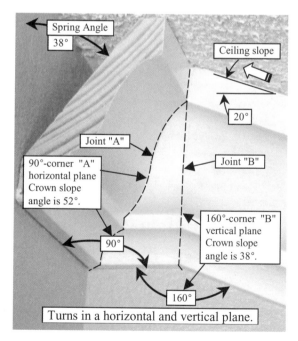

Turns in a horizontal and vertical plane.

Left-hand Inside Corner Template, Vertical Plane

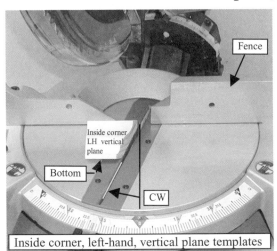

Inside corner, left-hand, vertical plane templates

To cut your left-hand template for an inside corner, vertical plane, place the crown face up with the top of the crown next to the fence. Rotate the miter table clockwise to 18.1° and tilt the blade to the left to 13.6°.

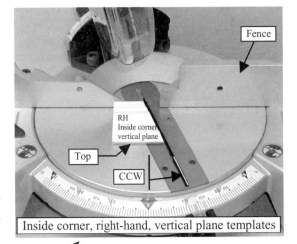

Inside corner, right-hand, vertical plane templates

Note: If you are using a miter saw, use the instructions for the Miter Table© in Chapter 3, page 24, to make your templates.

Right-hand Inside Corner Template, Vertical Plane

To cut your right-hand template for an inside corner, vertical plane, place the crown face up with the bottom of the crown next to the fence, the miter rotated counter-clockwise to 18.1°, and the blade tilted to the left to 13.6°.

You now have all the templates you need. You should have a set for inside and outside corners for turns in a horizontal/ ceiling plane, and a set for inside and outside corners for turns in a vertical plane. You will be able to use your set of templates for a horizontal plane to make turns in the ceiling plane, since the two are the same.

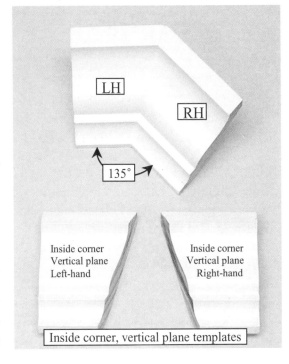

Inside corner, vertical plane templates

Let's take time here to review what we have done so far in this chapter. You should now understand the three planes in which you can turn the crown. They are **horizontal plane**, **vertical plane**, and **ceiling plane**. You should also know how to determine the **crown slope angle** for each of the turns in each of the three planes. You should know what the crown spring angle is and how to check it, making sure which crown you are using. What we have not covered in detail is turning the crown in the plane of the ceiling. There are **pros** and **cons** for turning the crown in the ceiling plane. Sometimes it is beneficial and sometimes it is not. We will address this later in this chapter. Most of your cathedral crown turns should be done in the **horizontal plane** and the **vertical plane**. This will prevent changing the spring angle. In other words, **if you are using crown with a spring angle of 38°, the angle from the back of the crown to the wall will remain 38° as long as you only turn in a horizontal or vertical plane**. As we progress through this chapter, I will provide examples of when it is better to turn the crown in the ceiling plane. Now let's take our set of templates and install some crown on a cathedral/vaulted ceiling.

Basic Cathedral/Vaulted Ceilings

This is a cathedral ceiling where the room is rectangular and the ceiling is sloped from two opposite walls to a peak in the center of the room. This model has a ceiling with a 20° slope. I am using 52°/38° crown molding (spring angle is 38°). I have made corner turns only in the horizontal plane and the vertical plane. Again, you should try to make turns in only these two planes.

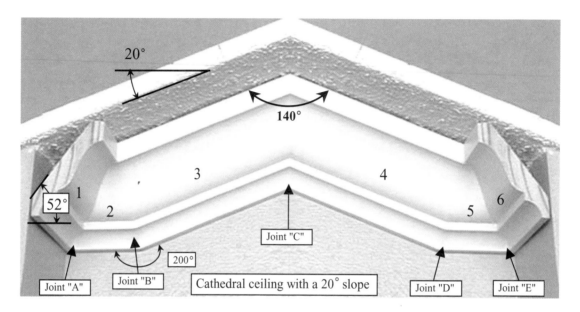

Cathedral ceiling with a 20° slope

Let's start this room with crown piece #1 and work from left to right. I will provide the details of how to get the miter and blade tilt for each crown joint. You should follow along with your Crown Molding Table©.

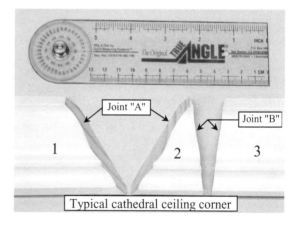

Typical cathedral ceiling corner

Joint "A" is an inside corner turn in the horizontal plane, corner angle = 90°, crown slope angle = 52°. Use your templates for a horizontal plane, inside corner. The miter angle = 31.6° and the blade tilt = 33.9°.

Joint "B" is an outside corner turn in the vertical plane, corner angle = 200° (ceiling slope = 20°), crown slope angle = 38°. (Remember, the crown slope angle is the angle from the back of the crown to the plane in which you are turning your crown.) Use your templates for a vertical plane, outside corner. The miter angle = 7.9° and the blade tilt = 6.1°.

You are probably wondering how I was able to measure and obtain a corner angle of 200° for joint "B" when there is not a 200° corner to measure. The 200° corner angle is a calculated value. To get this value, measure the angle in the **vertical plane** with the blades of the True Angle® tool placed against the wall and the ceiling (see illustration to the right). You get a measurement of 110° for a 20° sloping ceiling (90° + 20° ceiling slope = 110°). To obtain the corner angle for joint "B", add 90° to the 110° to get 200°. You will also need to do the same for joint "D".

Joint "C" is an inside corner turn in the vertical plane, corner angle = 140°, crown slope angle = 38°. Use your templates for a vertical plane, inside corner. The miter angle = 16.0° and the blade tilt = 12.2°.

Joint "D" is an outside corner turn in the vertical plane, corner angle = 200° (ceiling slope = 20°), crown slope angle = 38°. Use your templates for a vertical plane, outside corner. The miter angle = 7.9° and the blade tilt = 6.1°. Notice joints "B" and "D" have the same settings for miter and blade tilt angles.

Joint "E" is an inside corner turn in the horizontal plane, corner angle = 90°, crown slope angle = 52°. Use your templates for a horizontal plane, inside corner. The miter angle = 31.6° and the blade tilt = 33.9°. This is also the same as joint "A".

The model I built for the above example has true 90° corners. **Your house most likely does not!** That is why I recommend measuring every corner with your True Angle® tool. Place your tool flat in the plane in which you are making the turn to get the corner angle. Here I am measuring the corner angle of joint "C" in the above picture. The True Angle® is placed in the vertical plane and the blades of the tool are held against the ceiling. Tighten the tension screw and read the corner angle.

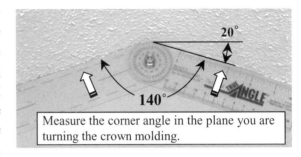

Measure the corner angle in the plane you are turning the crown molding.

Everything we have covered so far can be summarized as follows: Measure the corner angle with the True Angle® (placed in the plane in which you are making the turn). Determine the crown slope angle (angle from the back of the crown to the plane you are turning the crown). Then use the corner angle and crown slope angle in the Crown Molding Table©, Compound Miter Chart©, or the Miter Excel Program© to get the miter and blade tilt angles. Set your saw and make the perfect cut.

Cathedral/Vaulted and Horizontal Ceiling

In this example, our cathedral/vaulted ceiling turns into a horizontal ceiling. This is no different from the above example. Simply place your True Angle® in the vertical plane and measure the corner angle. The corner angle measures 140°. Use your templates for a vertical plane, inside corner. The crown slope angle is 38°. From this you can see the miter angle = 16.0° and the blade tilt = 12.2°.

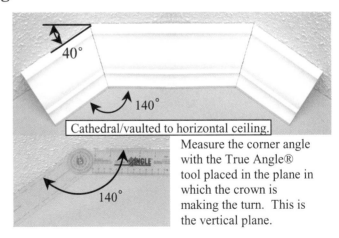

Cathedral/vaulted to horizontal ceiling.

Measure the corner angle with the True Angle® tool placed in the plane in which the crown is making the turn. This is the vertical plane.

Notice we have not made any turns of the crown molding in the ceiling plane. All turns have been either in the horizontal plane or the vertical plane. Also, the crown molding we have used so far has had a spring angle of 38°.

Cathedral/Vaulted Ceiling, Wall Makes a Turn

This example will further illustrate turning the crown in only the horizontal and vertical planes. In this example, we are working from left to right. Crown piece #1 is going up (left to right) along a cathedral/vaulted ceiling which has a slope of 10°. Instead of running into a vertical wall, the wall makes a 45° turn (135° corner angle). Here we must make three turns of the crown to get through this corner. The first turn is in the vertical plane (joint "A"), the second turn is in the horizontal plane (joint "B"), and the third turn is again in the vertical plane (joint "C").

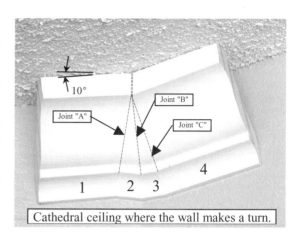

Cathedral ceiling where the wall makes a turn.

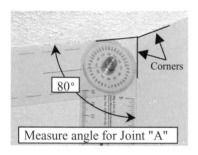

Measure angle for Joint "A"

Joint "A" is an inside corner turn in the vertical plane, corner angle = 170°, crown slope angle = 38°. Use your templates for a vertical plane, inside corner. The miter angle = 3.9° and the blade tilt = 3.1°. The corner angle for joint "A" is calculated. Measure the angle as shown, then add 90° (80°+90°=170°).

Joint "B" is an inside corner turn in the horizontal plane, corner angle = 135°, crown slope angle = 52°. Use your templates for a horizontal plane, inside corner. The miter angle = 14.3° and the blade tilt = 17.6°. Measure the corner angle of the two walls for joint "B" in the horizontal plane where the bottom of the crown will be placed.

Joint "C" is an outside corner turn in the vertical plane, corner angle = 188° (98°+90°=188°), crown slope angle = 38°. Use your templates for a vertical plane, outside corner. The miter angle = 3.2° and the blade tilt = 2.5°. Measure the angle as shown, then add 90° (98°+90°=188°).

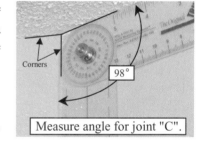

Measure angle for joint "C".

Use quick-setting glue or epoxy to join the small pieces of crown together.

Pros and Cons for Cathedral/Vaulted Ceiling Turns
Crown Molding Turns in the Ceiling Plane

Let's begin with an example of wrapping a column with crown. In this example, we are installing the crown horizontally (left to right) along a cathedral ceiling and we come to a column. (The column could be a bookcase, fireplace, cabinet, short wall, or any other extension into the room.)

If you wrap the column using turns in the horizontal plane and the vertical plane only, you will have to cut a wedge-shaped piece of trim to fill the void between the top of the crown and the ceiling at joint "D". There are easier ways, which we will cover next.

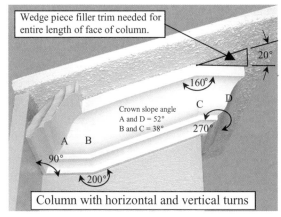

Wedge piece filler trim needed for entire length of face of column.

Crown slope angle
A and D = 52°
B and C = 38°

Column with horizontal and vertical turns

For our first example (below), we have turned the two outside corners of the column in the ceiling plane.

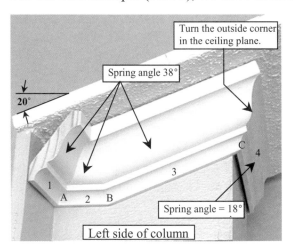

Turn the outside corner in the ceiling plane.

Spring angle 38°

Spring angle = 18°

Left side of column

Notice the spring angle of crown piece #4 (to the left) is 18° (38°-20° ceiling slope). The gap at the bottom of #4 will have to be caulked. Remember earlier when I said there were pros and cons associated with turning your crown in the ceiling plane? In this case, the pro is that you do not need to hand cut and fit a wedge piece to place above the crown. The con is that now you have to caulk the gap at the bottom of crown piece #4. This particular method is better suited for long wall partitions or offsets in the wall where crown piece #4 is fairly short and crown piece #3 is long.

To measure the corner angle in the ceiling plane, place your True Angle® flat against the ceiling. The corner angle is 270° and the crown slope angle for joint "C" is 52°. From the Crown Molding Table©, the miter angle = 31.6° and the blade tilt = 33.9°. **(Do not assume your corners are square. Use your True Angle® tool!)**

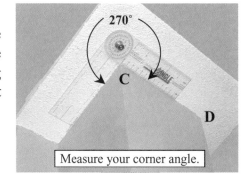

270°

Measure your corner angle.

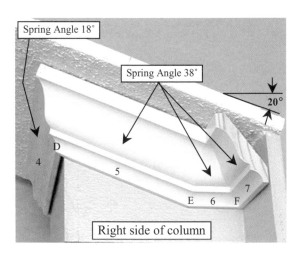

Spring Angle 18°

Spring Angle 38°

20°

Right side of column

Here is the right side of the column. The crown has returned to the correct position for #5 (bottom of crown rests firmly against the wall and the spring angle is 38°). It can be continued as shown. To get the miter and blade tilt angles for joint "D", measure the corner angle as shown above and use 52° as the crown slope angle. Use your outside corner templates for a horizontal/ceiling plane. (Remember, the horizontal and ceiling plane template sets are the same.)

Crown Molding Turns in the Ceiling Plane, Horizontal Wall

This is the best way to wrap a column. I am using the same model as before, except I have installed the crown differently. The crown runs horizontally (left to right) along the top of the wall of a 20° sloping cathedral ceiling, then we come to a column. (Again, the column could be a bookcase, fireplace, cabinet, short wall, or any other extension into the room.) This time we will make all four turns in the ceiling plane.

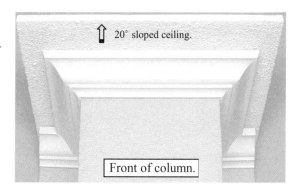

20° sloped ceiling.

Front of column.

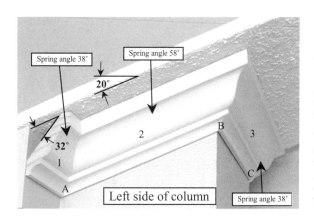

Spring angle 38°

Spring angle 58°

20°

32°

Left side of column

Spring angle 38°

Crown piece #1 has a spring angle of 38° with the bottom of the crown resting firmly against the wall. Since we will turn the crown in the ceiling plane, the crown slope angle for joint "A" is 32° (52°-20°ceiling slope = 32°). Place your True Angle® against the ceiling (in the plane of the ceiling) and measure the corner angle for joint "A" (let's assume 92°). Using the corner angle for joint "A" as 92° and a crown slope angle of 32°, you can get the miter and blade tilt angles from the Compound Miter Chart© or the Miter Excel Program©. The miter angle = 39.3° and the blade tilt = 21.6°.

Notice I did not mention the Crown Molding Table©. That's because the Crown Molding Table© does not contain the needed information. Ceilings vary in slope so much that it would take dozens of tables to cover all of the possibilities. I have included the Compound Miter Chart© at the end of this chapter. You can also purchase a plastic laminated Compound Miter Chart© and the Miter Excel Program© through our website. Now let's continue.

Joint "A" is now complete. The spring angle for crown piece #2 is 58° (38°+20° ceiling slope = 58°). Remember the pros and cons. This is a con. Crown piece #2 and crown piece #4 both have a spring angle of 58°. That means the bottom of the crown for #2 and #4 are not resting against the wall but tilted outward 20°. The crown will look very good anyway and you have wrapped the column with only four corner turns. This is a pro.

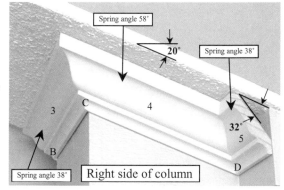

Spring angle 58°

20°

Spring angle 38°

32°

Spring angle 38°

Right side of column

The crown pieces that form joints A, B, C and D all have crown slope angles of 32° (angle from the back of the crown to the ceiling). Measure each corner angle in the ceiling plane with your True Angle® tool and use the Compound Miter Chart© or the Miter Excel Program© to obtain the correct miter and blade tilt angles needed for the perfect cut.

By now you should have a very good understanding of how to turn your crown in the ceiling plane. We have been working with a model of a column (above) that protrudes into the room while we are installing our crown horizontally. Now let's install crown around a column that protrudes into the room from the sloping wall of a cathedral/vaulted ceiling.

Crown Molding Turns in the Ceiling Plane, Sloping Wall

In this example, we are installing the crown from left to right up a 20° sloping cathedral/vaulted ceiling and come to a column. (Again, the column could be a bookcase, fireplace, cabinet, short wall, or any other extension into the room.) We will now make all four turns in the ceiling plane. The crown slope angle is 52°. You will see this example is almost like the previous example.

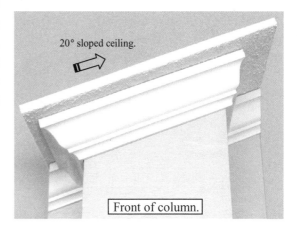

20° sloped ceiling.

Front of column.

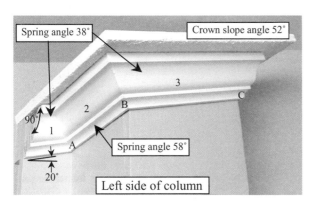

Spring angle 38° · Crown slope angle 52° · 90° · 20° · Spring angle 58° · Left side of column

Crown piece #1 has a spring angle of 38° with the bottom of the crown resting firmly against the wall. Since we will turn the crown in the ceiling plane, the crown slope angle for joint "A" is 52°. Place your True Angle® tool against the ceiling (in the plane of the ceiling) and measure the corner angle for joint "A" (let's assume 92°). Using the corner angle for joint "A" as 92° and a crown slope angle of 52°, you can

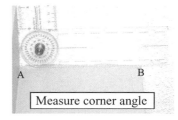

Measure corner angle

get the miter and blade tilt angles from the Crown Molding Table©, Compound Miter Chart© or the Miter Excel Program©. The miter angle = 30.7° and the blade tilt = 33.2°. Do you remember which templates to use? For corners "A" and "D", use your horizontal/cathedral plane templates for an inside corner. For corners "B" and "C", use your horizontal/cathedral plane templates for an outside corner.

The Crown Molding Table© can be used for this example because the table has the miter and blade tilt angles for a 52° crown slope angle.

The crown pieces that form joints A, B, C and D all have a crown slope angle of 52°. Measure each corner angle in the ceiling plane with your True Angle® and use the Crown Molding Table© or the Miter Excel Program© to obtain the correct miter and blade tilt angles needed for the perfect cut.

Notice the bottom of crown pieces #2 and #4 are not resting flush against the wall. This is, of course, one of the drawbacks of turning the crown in the ceiling plane. However, if you made all corner turns in the horizontal and vertical planes, it would be very difficult, taking quite a few more cuts and crown pieces to wrap the column. The bottom of crown piece #4 will have to be caulked.

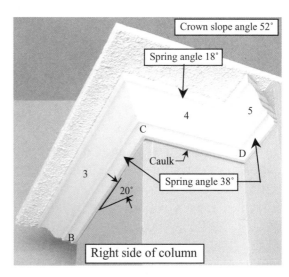

Crown slope angle 52° · Spring angle 18° · Caulk · Spring angle 38° · 20° · Right side of column

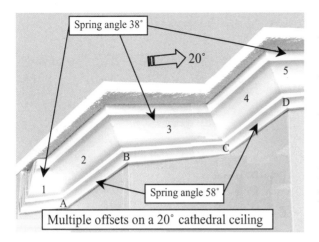

Spring angle 38°

20°

5

4

D

3

2

B

C

1

A

Multiple offsets on a 20° cathedral ceiling

Spring angle 58°

Here is another example where (working left to right) we are running the crown up a 20° sloped ceiling and have two offsets in the wall. Do exactly the same as in the previous examples. Measure the corner angles of corners A, B, C, and D by placing your True Angle® in the ceiling plane. The crown slope angle is 52° for all four corners. Get the miter and blade tilt angles from the Crown Molding Table©, Compound Miter Chart© or the Miter Excel Program©. Set your saw and make the perfect cut.

In this example (photo to the right), we are installing the crown (left to right) horizontally along a 17° sloping cathedral ceiling. We come to a recessed bay window that has a 225° outside corner and a horizontal ceiling. The first thing we want to do is turn the crown in the ceiling plane. Joint "A" will turn the crown down until the top of the crown comes to the horizontal ceiling. Joint "B" will turn the crown in the vertical plane, then continue horizontally.

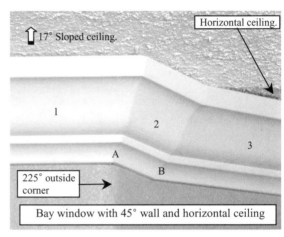

17° Sloped ceiling.

Horizontal ceiling.

1

2

3

A

B

225° outside corner

Bay window with 45° wall and horizontal ceiling

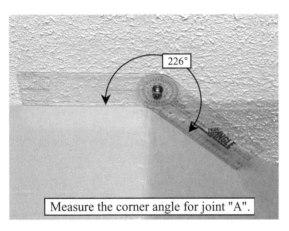

226°

Measure the corner angle for joint "A".

To measure the corner angle for joint "A", place your True Angle® in the ceiling plane as shown. We get a corner angle for joint "A" of 226° (outside corner). Note the right-hand blade of the tool is not against the horizontal ceiling. What is the crown slope angle? We are using 38° spring angle crown so the angle between the back of the crown and the ceiling, in this case, is 35° (52°-17° = 35°). The Crown Molding Table© does not have a 35° crown slope angle column so the information was obtained from the Compound Miter Chart©.

For joint "A", from the Compound Miter Chart© or the Miter Excel Program©, the miter = 19.17° and blade tilt = 12.95°. (Use your horizontal/ceiling plane, outside corner templates.)

To measure the corner angle for joint "B", place your True Angle® in the vertical plane as shown. We get 191°. What is the crown slope angle? We are turning the crown in the vertical plane for joint "B". The crown slope angle is 38°. From the Crown Molding Table©, Compound Miter Chart© or the Miter Excel Program©, you get miter = 4.3° and the blade tilt = 3.4°. (Use your vertical plane, outside corner templates.)

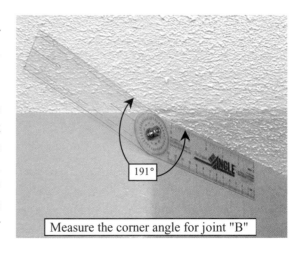

191°

Measure the corner angle for joint "B"

If your house has cathedral/vaulted ceilings and you have walls that are of various angles, you will probably have some conditions where you will not be able to turn the crown in the plane of the ceiling. In this example (photo to the right), the crown is running from left to right on a horizontal wall of a cathedral ceiling. The bay window has a horizontal ceiling. Crown piece #1 and crown piece #3 have about a ½" elevation difference. To make this elevation change, make a turn in the vertical plane, joint "A". Joint "A" is an inside corner of 135° and has a crown slope angle of 38°.

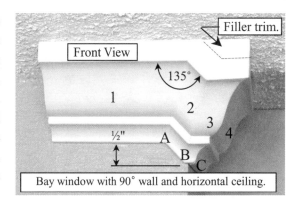

Bay window with 90° wall and horizontal ceiling.

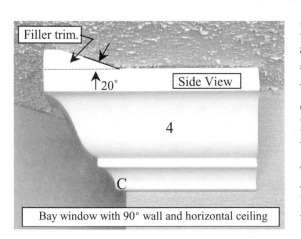

Bay window with 90° wall and horizontal ceiling

From the Crown Molding Table© in the 38° crown slope angle column, you get miter angle = 18.1° and the blade tilt = 13.6°. To turn back horizontally, you need to make another turn in the vertical plane, joint "B". Joint "B" is a 225° outside corner with a crown slope angle of 38°. This will have the same miter and blade tilt angles as joint "A". At this point, you are at the same elevation as crown piece #4. Joint "C" is a 270° outside corner in the horizontal plane. Joint "C" has a crown slope angle of 52°. From the Crown Molding Table© you get the miter angle = 31.6° and the blade tilt angle = 33.9°.

After you have installed (glue with fast-setting epoxy) the four pieces of crown around the corner, make a small filler trim piece. You can use a piece of 1" 90° corner trim from which to cut the filler piece. Glue the filler piece in place, caulking when necessary, to get a smooth surface, then paint.

Summary and Review

Installing crown molding on a cathedral/vaulted ceiling is not complicated. All you have to do is remember the few basic rules for making a turn with your crown molding.

To make the perfect crown molding joint:

1. Measure the corner angle with your True Angle® in the plane in which you are turning the crown and determine the correct crown slope angle (angle from the back of the crown to the plane in which you are turning the crown).
2. Get the miter and blade tilt angles from the Crown Molding Table©, Compound Miter Chart©, or the Miter Excel Program©.
3. Use your templates as a guide, set the saw, and make the perfect cut.

By now you have mastered the use of the True Angle® tool and can measure any corner angle in any one of the three planes in which you can turn the crown. The only other bit of information you need is the crown slope angle. I would like to review this with you at this time. Look at the two examples on pages 46 and 47. The first one, with the crown running horizontally at the top of the wall, has a crown slope angle of 32°. The second example, in which the crown is running along the sloped cathedral ceiling, has a crown slope angle of 52°. Remember the definition? The **crown slope angle** is the angle measured from the back of the crown to the plane in which you are turning the crown.

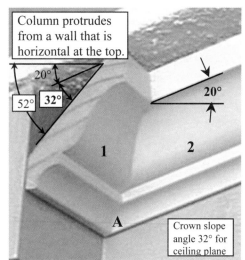

Column protrudes from a wall that is horizontal at the top.

20°
52° 32°
1   2
20°
A
Crown slope angle 32° for ceiling plane

For an upward sloping 20° ceiling, the crown slope angle for crown piece #1 in the ceiling plane is 32° (52°-20° = 32°). As long as you continue turning the crown in the ceiling plane, the crown slope angle does not change. However, the spring angle switches from 38° to 58° (38°+20° = 58°) and then from 58° to 38° each time you make a 90° turn. Use the Compound Miter Chart© to get the miter and blade tilt angles.

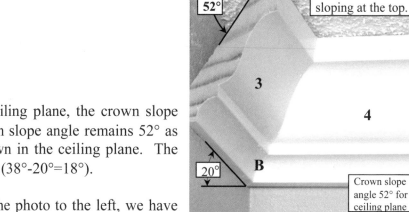

Column protrudes from a wall that is sloping at the top.

52°
3
4
20° B
Crown slope angle 52° for ceiling plane

If you turn crown piece #3 in the ceiling plane, the crown slope angle is 52° for joint "B". The crown slope angle remains 52° as long as you continue to turn the crown in the ceiling plane. The spring angle switches from 38° to 18° (38°-20°=18°).

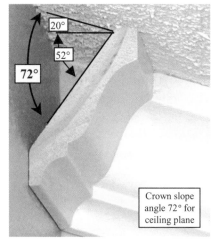

20°
52°
72°
Crown slope angle 72° for ceiling plane

In the photo to the left, we have a downward sloping 20° ceiling. The crown slope angle for the plane of the ceiling in this example is 72° (52°+20° = 72°). The spring angle switches from 38° to 18°. Use the Compound Miter Chart© for a 72° crown slope angle.

I cannot emphasize enough how important it is to make a set of templates for yourself. This is a full set of eight templates. Keep these with your compound miter saw.

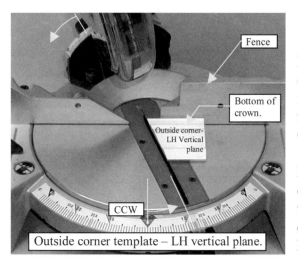

Fence
Bottom of crown.
Outside corner-LH Vertical plane
CCW
Outside corner template – LH vertical plane.

Find the template that matches the crown piece you want to cut. Place the template on your saw and adjust the saw to fit the template. Then set the miter and blade tilt angles that you obtained from the Crown Molding Table©, Compound Miter Chart© or the Miter Excel Program©.

For a free download of extra crown molding tables containing 10,800 saw settings (18 pages, PDF file), go to www.compoundmiter.com/extratables. These tables contain all the information found in the Compound Miter Chart on pages 51 and 52.

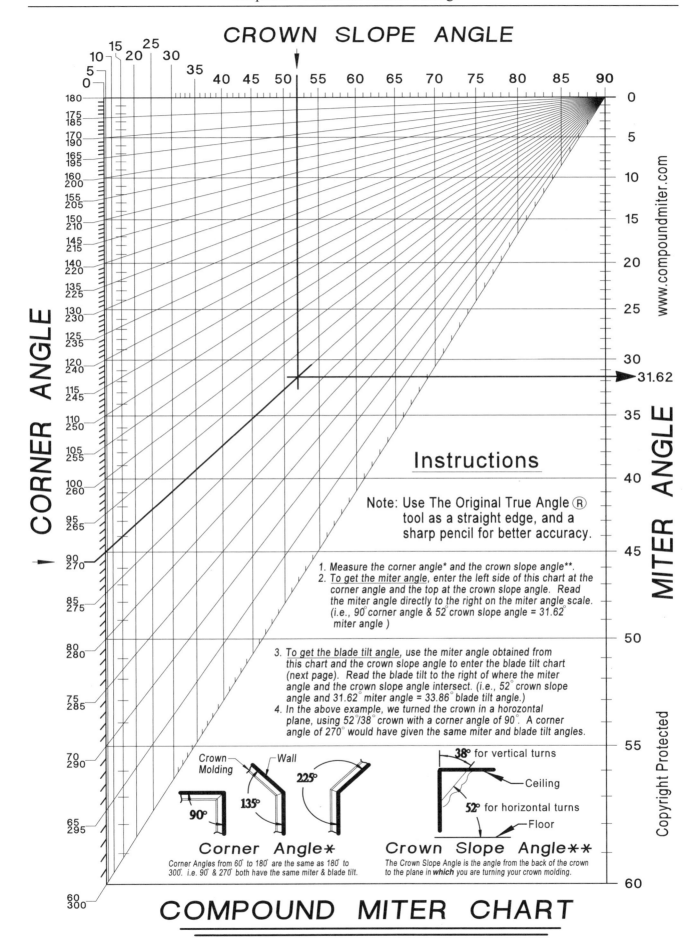

CROWN SLOPE ANGLE

CORNER ANGLE

MITER ANGLE

www.compoundmiter.com

31.62

Instructions

Note: Use The Original True Angle ® tool as a straight edge, and a sharp pencil for better accuracy.

1. Measure the corner angle* and the crown slope angle**.
2. To get the miter angle, enter the left side of this chart at the corner angle and the top at the crown slope angle. Read the miter angle directly to the right on the miter angle scale. (i.e., 90˚ corner angle & 52˚ crown slope angle = 31.62˚ miter angle)
3. To get the blade tilt angle, use the miter angle obtained from this chart and the crown slope angle to enter the blade tilt chart (next page). Read the blade tilt to the right of where the miter angle and the crown slope angle intersect. (i.e., 52˚ crown slope angle and 31.62˚ miter angle = 33.86˚ blade tilt angle.)
4. In the above example, we turned the crown in a horozontal plane, using 52˚/38˚ crown with a corner angle of 90˚. A corner angle of 270˚ would have given the same miter and blade tilt angles.

Crown Molding   Wall   225°   135°   90°

Corner Angle✱

Corner Angles from 60˚ to 180˚ are the same as 180˚ to 300˚. i.e. 90˚ & 270˚ both have the same miter & blade tilt.

38° for vertical turns   Ceiling   52° for horizontal turns   Floor

Crown Slope Angle✱✱

The Crown Slope Angle is the angle from the back of the crown to the plane in **which** you are turning your crown molding.

Copyright Protected

COMPOUND MITER CHART

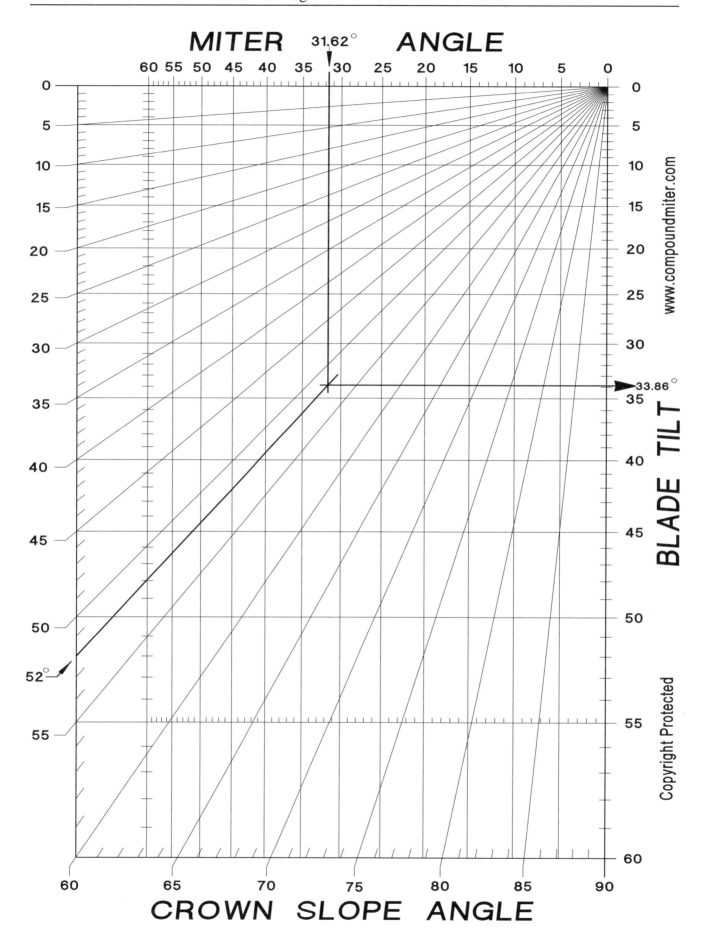

MITER   31.62°   ANGLE

BLADE TILT

CROWN SLOPE ANGLE

www.compoundmiter.com

Copyright Protected

33.86°

52°

Bullnose (Radius) Corners

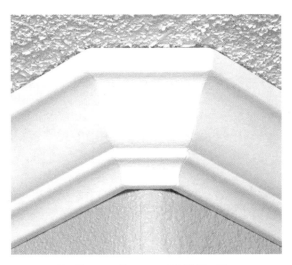

Bullnose Corner, 3/4" Radius

There are two outside corner construction methods. The first is where the corner comes to an abrupt edge, then makes a turn. We have dealt with this method throughout this book. The second method is called a bullnose (radius) corner.

There are three sizes of bullnose corner caps available, 1/2", 3/4" and 1-1/2" radius. The most common size used for residential construction is 3/4". If you have 1/2" or 3/4" radius corners, use one crown piece. If you have 1-1/2" radius corners, use two crown pieces.

The two drawings below show the typical construction of a bullnose corner and how the crown is wrapped around a 270° outside corner using one crown piece (1/2" or 3/4" radius bullnose).

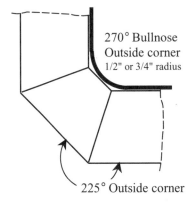

Bullnose Corner, 1-1/2" Radius

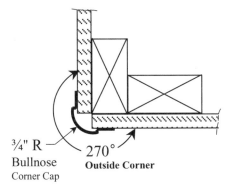

¾" R Bullnose Corner Cap

270° Outside Corner

Typical bullnose corner construction

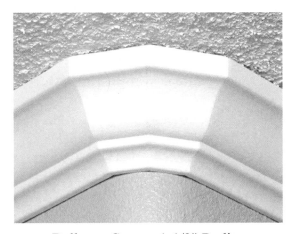

270° Bullnose Outside corner 1/2" or 3/4" radius

225° Outside corner

Using 1, 2 or 3 Crown Pieces
Outside Corner Angle

Notice in the drawing to the right, the bullnose corner angle is 270°, yet the outside corner angle we will use in the Crown Molding Table© is 225°. (Table 1 on page 55 will provide these angles.)

To get the miter and blade tilt angles for these cuts, use the Crown Molding Table© or the Miter Excel Program©. For this example, enter the Crown Molding Table© at an outside corner angle of 225°. Go across to the crown slope angle you have and read the miter and blade tilt angles. For horizontal turns of 52°/38° crown, you have a crown slope angle of 52°, giving a miter angle = 14.3° and the blade tilt = 17.6°. For 45°/45° crown, the crown slope angle is 45°, giving a miter angle = 16.3° and the blade tilt = 15.7°.

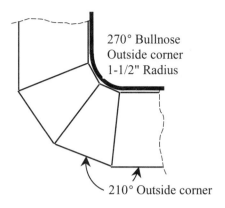

270° Bullnose
Outside corner
1-1/2" Radius

210° Outside corner

If you have 1-1/2" radius bullnose corners, use two small pieces of crown to make the corner turn. For a 270° outside corner, 1-1/2" bullnose, use 210° as the corner angle (Table 1).

Making a corner turn with two crown pieces is a little more difficult. You might make a sample using one piece and then a sample using two pieces and see which you prefer. To get the miter and blade tilt angles using two pieces, just repeat the instructions above using 210° as the corner angle. A 52° crown slope angle will give you a miter angle = 9.4° and blade tilt = 11.8°. A 45° crown slope angle will give you a miter angle = 10.7° and blade tilt = 10.6°.

If you have bullnose corners with a radius greater than 1-1/2", use three pieces of crown. For a 270° outside bullnose corner with three crown pieces, the corner angle would be 202.5°.

If you have bullnose corners that are not exactly 270°, use Table 1 to get the actual outside corner angle needed for the Crown Molding Table©. To use Table 1, simply measure the corner angle of the bullnose corner with your True Angle®. Locate that angle in the column labeled "Measured Corner Angle of Your Bullnose Corner". Then read across to the column for the number of crown pieces used and get the corner angle needed for the Crown Molding Table©.

As an example, let's use the 270° outside bullnose corner from our example above. Look at Table 1 and find 270° as the bullnose corner angle. For one crown piece we see that the corner angle would be 225°, for two crown pieces it would be 210°, and for three it would be 202.5°. What if you measured the bullnose corner angle to be 225° and you wanted to use one crown piece? What corner angle would you use in the Crown Molding Table©? (Answer: 202.5°)

Let's do another example. This time we have measured our bullnose corner angle to be 286°. What would be the actual corner angle needed for the Crown Molding Table© if we wanted to use 1, 2, or 3 crown pieces? (Answer: 1 piece = 233°; 2 pieces = 215.3°; 3 pieces = 206.5)

You should now have a good understanding of how to get the corner angle needed for the Crown Molding Table© in order to get the miter and blade tilt angles for your bullnose corner.

Width to Cut Each Crown Piece

Now that you have the miter and blade tilt angles needed, you also need to know how wide to cut the bottoms of each crown piece (the bottom of the crown that actually rests against the bullnose corner). For that, you will need to measure the radius of your bullnose corner.

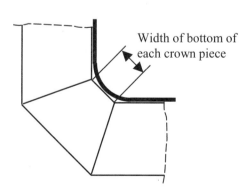

Width of bottom of each crown piece

The width of each crown piece varies as the bullnose corner angle, the number of pieces, and/or the bullnose radius changes. Table 1 and Table 2 (pages 55 and 56) will provide you with the additional information you need to cut your bullnose crown molding.

The radius of a 270° bullnose corner can easily be determined by placing your True Angle® on the corner and measuring as shown. If your bullnose corners are not 270° ± 5°, draw a series of arcs on stiff paper with radiuses from 1/2" to 1-1/2" in 1/16" increments using a compass. Start with the smallest radius and cut along the line with a pair of scissors. Then fit this to your bullnose. If it does not fit, cut the next larger radius and continue trying until you find the radius that fits your bullnose corner.

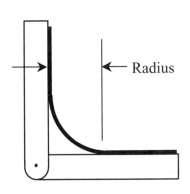

← Radius

Table 1 - Outside Corner Angle (Bullnose Corner)							
Measured Corner Angle of your Bullnose Corner (degrees)	This is the corner angle to use in the Crown Molding Table for your measured bullnose corner angle and the number of pieces used. Crown Pieces Used			Measured Corner Angle of your Bullnose Corner (degrees)	This is the corner angle to use in the Crown Molding Table for your measured bullnose corner angle and the number of pieces used. Crown Pieces Used		
	1	2	3		1	2	3
190	185.0	183.3	182.5	272	226.0	210.7	203.0
192	186.0	184.0	183.0	274	227.0	211.3	203.5
194	187.0	184.7	183.5	276	228.0	212.0	204.0
196	188.0	185.3	184.0	278	229.0	212.7	204.5
198	189.0	186.0	184.5	280	230.0	213.3	205.0
200	190.0	186.7	185.0	282	231.0	214.0	205.5
202	191.0	187.3	185.5	284	232.0	214.7	206.0
204	192.0	188.0	186.0	286	233.0	215.3	206.5
206	193.0	188.7	186.5	288	234.0	216.0	207.0
208	194.0	189.3	187.0	290	235.0	216.7	207.5
210	195.0	190.0	187.5	292	236.0	217.3	208.0
212	196.0	190.7	188.0	294	237.0	218.0	208.5
214	197.0	191.3	188.5	296	238.0	218.7	209.0
216	198.0	192.0	189.0	298	239.0	219.3	209.5
218	199.0	192.7	189.5	300	240.0	220.0	210.0
220	200.0	193.3	190.0	302	241.0	220.7	210.5
222	201.0	194.0	190.5	304	242.0	221.3	211.0
224	202.0	194.7	191.0	306	243.0	222.0	211.5
226	203.0	195.3	191.5	308	244.0	222.7	212.0
228	204.0	196.0	192.0	310	245.0	223.3	212.5
230	205.0	196.7	192.5	312	246.0	224.0	213.0
232	206.0	197.3	193.0	314	247.0	224.7	213.5
234	207.0	198.0	193.5	316	248.0	225.3	214.0
236	208.0	198.7	194.0	318	249.0	226.0	214.5
238	209.0	199.3	194.5	320	250.0	226.7	215.0
240	210.0	200.0	195.0	322	251.0	227.3	215.5
242	211.0	200.7	195.5	324	252.0	228.0	216.0
244	212.0	201.3	196.0	326	253.0	228.7	216.5
246	213.0	202.0	196.5	328	254.0	229.3	217.0
248	214.0	202.7	197.0	330	255.0	230.0	217.5
250	215.0	203.3	197.5	332	256.0	230.7	218.0
252	216.0	204.0	198.0	334	257.0	231.3	218.5
254	217.0	204.7	198.5	336	258.0	232.0	219.0
256	218.0	205.3	199.0	338	259.0	232.7	219.5
258	219.0	206.0	199.5	340	260.0	233.3	220.0
260	220.0	206.7	200.0	342	261.0	234.0	220.5
262	221.0	207.3	200.5	344	262.0	234.7	221.0
264	222.0	208.0	201.0	346	263.0	235.3	221.5
266	223.0	208.7	201.5	348	264.0	236.0	222.0
268	224.0	209.3	202.0	350	265.0	236.7	222.5
270	225.0	210.0	202.5				

http://www.compoundmiter.com, a Quint Group company, since March 2000

To get the width of the bottom of each crown piece, enter Table 2 at the "Measured Corner Angle of your Bullnose Corner" and move across to the column for the number of crown pieces. For example: 240° bullnose corner, 2 crown pieces = 0.353. Now multiply 0.353 by the radius of the bullnose corner. If your radius is 3/4", the width = 0.353 x 0.75" = 0.26". (I have included a fraction to decimal conversion table in Chapter 17.)

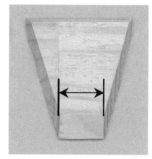

Width of each crown piece

Due to the small size of the crown piece, you will not be able to use nails. I have found it very useful to glue/epoxy the small pieces together (use fast setting), then glue/epoxy the remaining pieces when making the final installation. I would recommend that nails in the long sections of the crown not be any closer to the joint than 3" (pre-drill nail holes).

Table 2 - Bottom Width of Crown Piece (Bullnose Corner)

Measured Corner Angle of your Bullnose Corner (degrees)	Use this number and multiply by the radius of your bullnose corner to get the width of the bottom of each crown piece. Crown Pieces Used			Measured Corner Angle of your Bullnose Corner (degrees)	Use this number and multiply by the radius of your bullnose corner to get the width of the bottom of each crown piece. Crown Pieces Used		
	1	2	3		1	2	3
190	0.087	0.058	0.044	272	0.849	0.548	0.407
192	0.105	0.070	0.052	274	0.870	0.561	0.416
194	0.122	0.081	0.061	276	0.890	0.573	0.425
196	0.140	0.093	0.070	278	0.911	0.586	0.434
198	0.157	0.105	0.079	280	0.933	0.599	0.443
200	0.175	0.116	0.087	282	0.954	0.611	0.453
202	0.193	0.128	0.096	284	0.975	0.624	0.462
204	0.210	0.140	0.105	286	0.997	0.637	0.471
206	0.228	0.152	0.114	288	1.019	0.650	0.480
208	0.246	0.163	0.122	290	1.041	0.663	0.489
210	0.263	0.175	0.131	292	1.063	0.676	0.499
212	0.281	0.187	0.140	294	1.086	0.689	0.508
214	0.299	0.198	0.149	296	1.109	0.702	0.517
216	0.317	0.210	0.157	298	1.132	0.715	0.527
218	0.335	0.222	0.166	300	1.155	0.728	0.536
220	0.353	0.234	0.175	302	1.178	0.741	0.545
222	0.371	0.246	0.184	304	1.202	0.754	0.555
224	0.389	0.257	0.193	306	1.226	0.768	0.564
226	0.407	0.269	0.201	308	1.250	0.781	0.573
228	0.425	0.281	0.210	310	1.274	0.795	0.583
230	0.443	0.293	0.219	312	1.299	0.808	0.592
232	0.462	0.305	0.228	314	1.324	0.822	0.602
234	0.480	0.317	0.237	316	1.349	0.835	0.611
236	0.499	0.329	0.246	318	1.375	0.849	0.621
238	0.517	0.341	0.254	320	1.400	0.863	0.631
240	0.536	0.353	0.263	322	1.427	0.877	0.640
242	0.555	0.365	0.272	324	1.453	0.890	0.650
244	0.573	0.377	0.281	326	1.480	0.904	0.660
246	0.592	0.389	0.290	328	1.507	0.918	0.669
248	0.611	0.401	0.299	330	1.535	0.933	0.679
250	0.631	0.413	0.308	332	1.563	0.947	0.689
252	0.650	0.425	0.317	334	1.591	0.961	0.698
254	0.669	0.437	0.326	336	1.620	0.975	0.708
256	0.689	0.449	0.335	338	1.649	0.990	0.718
258	0.708	0.462	0.344	340	1.678	1.004	0.728
260	0.728	0.474	0.353	342	1.708	1.019	0.738
262	0.748	0.486	0.362	344	1.739	1.034	0.748
264	0.768	0.499	0.371	346	1.769	1.049	0.758
266	0.788	0.511	0.380	348	1.801	1.063	0.768
268	0.808	0.523	0.389	350	1.833	1.078	0.778
270	0.828	0.536	0.398				

Now that we have all this information available to us, let's do a few examples using the illustrations to the right as a reference.

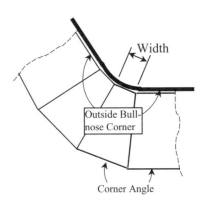

1ˢᵗ Example: 234° bullnose corner, 1-1/2" radius, and two crown pieces.
Enter Table 1 at 234° bullnose corner, then read across to the column for two crown pieces and get 198° as the corner angle. Use 198° in the Crown Molding Table (or the Miter Table© if using a miter saw) to get the miter and blade tilt angles. For 52°/38° crown, miter = 5.6° and blade tilt = 7.1°. For 45°/45° crown, miter = 6.4° and blade tilt = 6.4°. Go to Table 2 at 234° bullnose corner, then across to the column for two crown pieces to get 0.317. The width = 0.317 x 1.5" (radius) = 0.476".

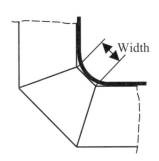

2ⁿᵈ Example: 264° bullnose corner, 3/4" radius, and one crown piece.
Enter Table 1 at 264° bullnose corner, then read across to the column for one crown piece and get 222° as the corner angle. Use 222° in the Crown Molding Table© (or the Miter Table© if using a miter saw) to get the miter and blade tilt angles. For 52°/38° crown, miter = 13.3° and blade tilt = 16.4°. For 45°/45° crown, miter = 15.2° and blade tilt = 14.7°. Go to Table 2 at 264° bullnose corner, then across to the column for one crown piece to get 0.768. The width = 0.768 x .75" (radius) = 0.576".

3ʳᵈ Example: 190° bullnose corner, 3/4" radius, and one crown piece.
From Table 1, the corner angle = 185°. From the Crown Molding Table© for 52°/38° crown, miter = 1.6° and blade tilt = 2°. For 45°/45° crown, miter = 1.8° and blade tilt = 1.8°. From Table 2, the width = 0.087 x 0.75" (radius) = 0.065".

I have presented Example 3 to illustrate a point. Notice how small the miter and blade tilt angles are and how narrow the width of the back of the crown is next to the bullnose corner. It would be a waste of time to cut crown pieces this small. You would just treat this corner as though it were a 190° standard (not a bullnose) outside corner. As a matter of fact, you will have small crown pieces for bullnose corners measuring less than 225° and will probably want to treat those as standard corners. Whatever you decide, you have the information to cut the crown for any outside bullnose corner you have.

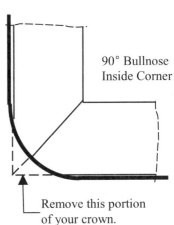

I have not mentioned anything so far about an inside bullnose corner. That's because you **cannot** wrap an inside bullnose corner. The two runs of crown along the wall interfere with the inside bullnose radius and must be trimmed as shown here. Typically, bullnose corner caps are applied to outside corners only. However, some builders will use inside corner caps as well.

Summary and Review

I have given a step-by-step approach to cutting the crown pieces for your bullnose corners. You will need your True Angle® tool, Tables 1 and 2, and the Crown Molding Table© to get the miter and blade tilt settings needed for your saw. If you have a non-standard crown, use the Compound Miter Chart© to obtain the miter and blade tilt angles.

Step 1. Decide if you want to install one crown piece or two crown pieces. Usually one crown piece is preferred for 1/2" to 3/4" radius bullnose corners and two crown pieces for 1-1/2" bullnose corners. I have provided the information in the tables for three crown pieces; however, I have never used three. If you have a corner radius greater than 1-1/2", you might want to use three crown pieces.

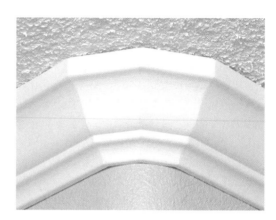

Step 2. Measure the bullnose corner angle with your True Angle®. The corner angle needed for the number of crown pieces used can be obtained from Table 1. Use this corner angle in the Crown Molding Table© to get the miter and blade tilt angles. The picture to the right is what your crown pieces will look like when using one crown piece. Use your horizontal/ceiling outside corner templates to help you set your saw.

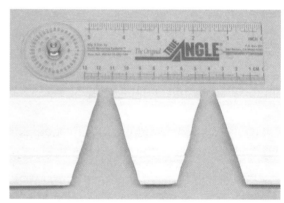

Step 3. Measure the radius of your bullnose corner using your True Angle® as described earlier, then use Table 2 to determine how wide to cut the bottom of each crown piece.

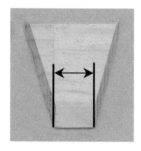

You should measure each bullnose radius to make sure they are all the same. When cutting the small crown piece, it is better to cut it a little too long at first, then trim to fit.

Cut and check each piece to make sure they all fit well.

Step 4. Glue or epoxy your corner together. When nailing the long piece of crown, do not nail any closer than 3" to the ends and pre-drill the nail hole first. If you prefer using hot glue to join the crown pieces together, I recommend using the type that requires a high-temperature glue gun. Check with your local craft/supply store for high-strength glue sticks.

Splicing/Joining Crown or Trim

Very often you will have a wall that is longer than a full length of crown or trim, or you will have several long pieces of crown remaining that you want to use instead of buying more full-length pieces. When this occurs, you can splice two or more pieces of crown or trim together to run the length you need. It is better to use full-length pieces and keep the splicing to a minimum, but sometimes it is not possible or economically feasible.

Cutting the Splice/Joint

When it is necessary to make a splice, you should set your miter angle to 30° and the blade tilt to 45° for a compound miter saw. I have found these angle settings to be the least noticeable when finished. If you are using a miter saw, set your miter angle to 45° with the bottom of the crown propped up on the fence (page 24). Make sure the total length of the pieces of crown you are going to splice is long enough to allow for trimming and fitting (at least 4 to 5 times the width of the crown you are using).

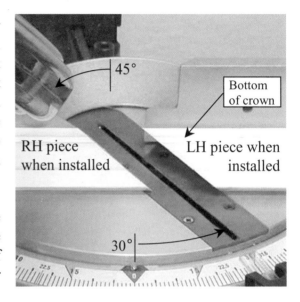

If you are installing your crown from right to left, cut the splice/joint as shown in the picture to the right, with the bottom of the crown against the fence and placed flat. If you are installing your crown from left to right, cut your splice with the top of the crown next to the fence.

It is better not to move or re-adjust the angles between cuts, but to cut both the left-hand piece and the right-hand piece using the exact same settings. This will assure a perfect joint alignment.

Installing the Splice/Joint

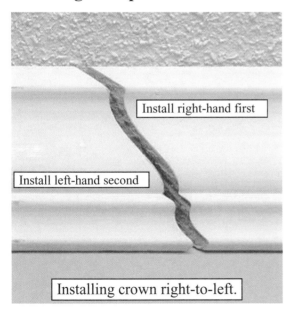

Install right-hand first

Install left-hand second

Installing crown right-to-left.

In this example, I am installing the crown from right to left. Install the right-hand piece first, then trim the left-hand piece to length from the corner end. Do not trim from the end that will be spliced.

Check-fit the second piece and continue trimming from the corner end until it fits.

When you have the second piece trimmed to the correct length, place a generous coating of wood glue to both surfaces of the splice. Install the second piece. Use a damp cloth or sponge to remove any excess glue.

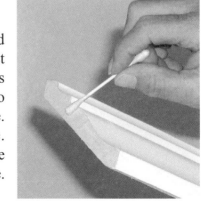

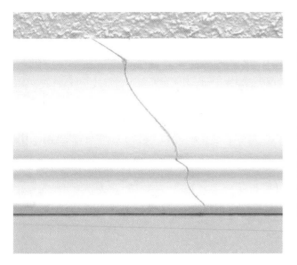

Here is the finished splice that is ready to receive a light coat of spackling and touch-up paint. For a smoother joint, lightly sand the spackling with 120-grit sandpaper before painting.

If you are installing trim such as baseboards or chair rails, cut the trim in the same manner and use a miter of 30° and a blade tilt of 45°. (If you are using a miter saw to cut your trim, set the miter to 45° and make the splice cut. See page 24.)

Summary and Review

When making a splice in crown or trim, you can vary the miter and blade tilt angles to your liking. I have used a miter of 30° and blade tilt of 45° with great success. I would recommend you never square cut a splice. You will have difficulties in getting a square cut splice not to show when finished.

Always cut both ends of the crown to form the splice joint without making any changes to your saw between cuts. This will give you the best fit.

I highly recommend you glue all splice joints. All wood tends to absorb or release moisture depending on its environment. A piece of crown that contains very little moisture will be slightly shorter than the same piece that is in a humid environment.

When nailing the splice, do not nail any closer than 3" to the splice without first drilling a small hole for the nail. This will prevent the crown or trim from splitting.

Crown Returns

Sometimes you may need to stop the crown at some location on the wall and not continue into a corner. For example, a doorway goes all the way to the ceiling and you do not want to carry the crown into the next room. You can stop short of the door entry. You could also make the initial turn and return the crown to the middle of the door jam face.

Cutting a Crown Return

A crown return is nothing more than making a 270° outside corner turn with your crown and butting it into the wall. Take a look at the picture to the right. Use your horizontal turn templates for an outside corner to align your saw and the miter and blade tilt angles for the type of crown you are using. Remember to always check the spring angle of your crown. If you are running your crown from left to right, as in this picture, cut the right-hand side of the outside corner so that you have a point at the bottom of the crown. If you are installing your crown from right to left, cut opposite.

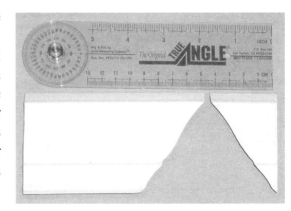

Installing a Crown Return

Install the crown return just as you would the rest of your crown. You should always place alignment marks along the wall as described in Chapter 4. This will ensure the crown is installed properly on the wall.

Glue the short return piece to the longer piece. You can also place some caulk on the end that butts into the wall to help hold it in place. When nailing the long piece of crown, do not nail any closer than 3" from the end.

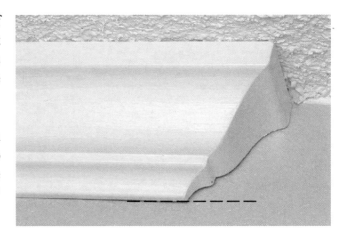

Summary and Review

A crown return is very much like the Cornice/Shelves in Chapter 10 where we simply return the crown back to the wall.

You can also return trim to the wall. If you are installing chair rail and want to stop midway on the wall, cut the trim as though you are turning an outside corner. Then cut a short piece to mate to the end of the chair rail and return it to the wall.

Caulking Crown Molding/Trim

Caulking your crown properly will make the difference between a good-looking job and a great-looking job. No matter how perfect your joints, paint will not bridge a seam. A light application of caulk will make your crown seem like it is molded into the wall as one solid piece.

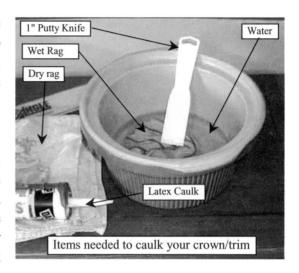

Items needed to caulk your crown/trim

Items You Will Need

You will need a bowl of water, 10-ounce tube of latex caulk, 9" caulking gun, 1" putty knife, and dry and wet rags. Use a good quality latex caulk. One tube will easily cover a medium-size room (15'x20'). Most latex caulks are inexpensive ($2 to $3 per tube) and carry a 25 to 35-year guarantee. If you are caulking outdoors, make sure the caulk is intended for exterior use. You will also need a light-weight spackling or painter's putty for the nail holes.

Using a Caulking Gun

For the beginner who has never used a caulking gun, let's review the basic parts and what they are for. This caulking gun is equipped with a spout cutter. Use this (or a sharp knife) to trim the tip of your caulk tube spout. The wire probe is used to puncture the aluminum foil seal located inside the spout at its base. Some caulk tubes do not have a seal. The wire probe will rotate 180° when not needed.

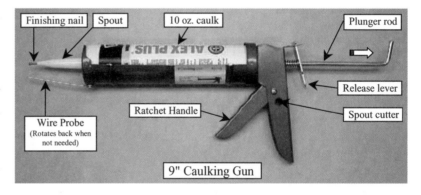

9" Caulking Gun

To insert your tube of caulk, press the release lever and pull the plunger rod all the way out. Place your caulk tube in the caulking gun and push the plunger rod in until it stops against the caulk tube. The ratchet handle, when squeezed, will build up pressure inside the caulk tube forcing the caulk out the spout. Apply a constant force to the ratchet handle while dispensing the caulk. The greater the force, the faster the caulk will flow from the spout.

When you have depressed the handle a full stroke, release it and apply pressure to the handle again. This will cause an even flow of caulk to be dispensed from the caulking gun. Any time you want to stop the flow of caulk, just press the release lever. **Note:** If you lay your caulking gun down without pressing the release lever, the caulk will continue to flow until the pressure inside the caulk tube decreases. Anytime you stop caulking for more than five minutes, insert a finishing nail in the spout to prevent the caulk from drying.

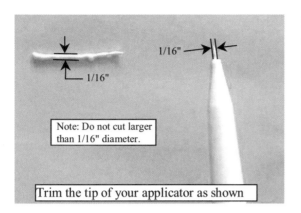

Note: Do not cut larger than 1/16" diameter.

Trim the tip of your applicator as shown

One of the most common mistakes made when caulking is cutting the end of the caulk tube too large. The tip should be trimmed straight across so that you have a 1/16" diameter hole in the end of the spout. If you cut the spout too large, you will be applying far too much caulk. This will make a big mess and waste a lot of caulk.

Caulking Top and Bottom of Crown/Trim

Let's start at the top. I am often asked what to do about gaps at the top of the crown due to the unevenness of the ceiling. Most often, the best and easiest thing to do is caulk the gap. Here is a gap that is almost 1/4" wide. Fill the void with caulk and you will never notice it when finished. Do not try to force the crown upward to fill the gap. The curve in the crown will be more noticeable than the caulk.

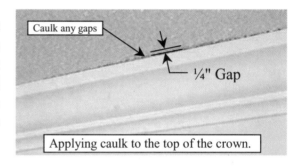

Caulk any gaps

¼" Gap

Applying caulk to the top of the crown.

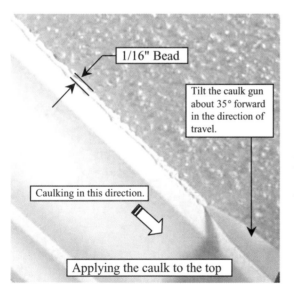

1/16" Bead

Tilt the caulk gun about 35° forward in the direction of travel.

Caulking in this direction.

Applying the caulk to the top

You can start caulking the top anywhere you wish. Place the caulk applicator at a 35° slant in the direction you will be going and keep constant pressure on the ratchet handle. Keep the caulking gun moving steadily and form a small bead as shown here. Only work about 5' at a time. After you have placed a 5' bead of caulk, stop and smooth the bead into the corner. If you go completely around the room and back to where you started, the caulk will have already dried to some extent.

In the picture to the right, I am smoothing the bead of caulk into the joint. To do this, drag your finger down the joint and evenly distribute the caulk into the joint. If there are any pinholes or voids where you have been, you can place a small amount of caulk over the void and smooth it over. Wipe the excess caulk from your finger every few feet. If you place too much caulk in the joint initially, you will have a lot to remove from your finger.

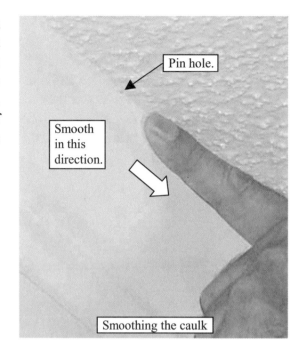

Pin hole.

Smooth in this direction.

Smoothing the caulk

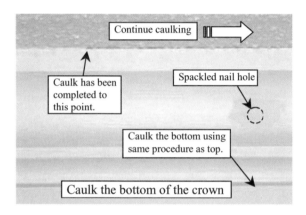

Continue caulking

Caulk has been completed to this point.

Spackled nail hole

Caulk the bottom using same procedure as top.

Caulk the bottom of the crown

Start the next 5' length where the smoothed caulk ends. Continue working your way around the top of the crown until you have completed the entire room. You are now ready to do the bottom. This is accomplished in exactly the same manner. After top and bottom caulking is completed, apply caulk to the joints of all inside and outside corners. To do this, just apply a small amount of caulk to the corner joints and wipe the excess off with the damp rag. I often use a cotton swab on the inside corners to help spread the caulk evenly. You have now completed the caulking and are ready to fill in the nail holes. ***Always paint your trim before cutting and installing it so you will only have to apply touch-up paint.***

Spackling Nail Holes

For the nail holes, it is better to use a light-weight spackling or painter's putty. These are better for nail holes because caulk shrinks as it dries leaving a small dimple. I prefer using light-weight spackling, because it is easier to apply and dries faster than putty. I find it easiest to apply a small amount of spackling to a piece of stiff paper or cardboard, and carry it around with me (instead of the can of spackling). Get about 1/4" of spackling in the center of your putty knife.

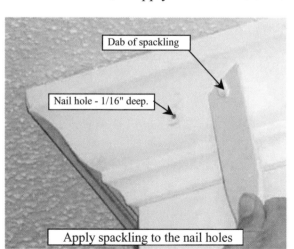

Dab of spackling

Nail hole - 1/16" deep.

Apply spackling to the nail holes

Start at any location and work your way around the room spackling each nail hole. Make sure all of the nails have been countersunk 1/16" deep. Do not sink the nails any deeper than 1/16". Too deep, and the nail might go through the crown.

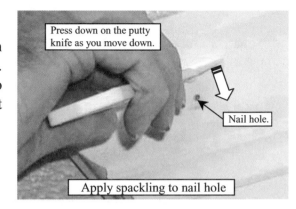

Press down on the putty knife as you move down.

Nail hole.

Apply spackling to nail hole

Place your putty knife above the nail hole and press down as you move the knife-edge down the face of the crown. This will force the spackling into the nail hole and will also leave a nice smooth clean surface behind the knife edge that can be painted over when dry.

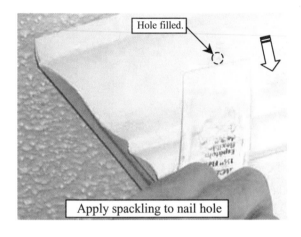

Hole filled.

Apply spackling to nail hole

It will not take long to get the hang of this, and the spackling will completely hide the nails. Between spackling every two nail holes, wipe the excess spackling from the knife edge and get another small dab in the center of the putty knife. You should have a completely smooth surface ready for touch-up paint once the spackling has dried. It is very important to keep everything clean as you work. Use the wet and dry rags to keep your hands and putty knife clean. Change your water often.

If you are installing dental crown or another type of crown/trim that does not have a smooth surface, use a cotton swab or equivalent item to apply a small amount of spackling in the nail hole and a damp rag to lightly remove any excess spackling.

Summary and Review
To caulk your crown molding or trim, you will need a 9" caulking gun, latex caulk, 1" putty knife, bowl of water, and wet and dry rags.

We discussed all of the parts of the 9" caulking gun and what each part is for. Remember to press the release lever every time you stop caulking. This will stop the flow of caulk. To caulk crown molding or trim, you should cut the caulk spout straight across to a 1/16" diameter opening.

Apply just enough caulk so you can smooth the joint evenly. Work only 5' at a time. Keep your putty knife and hands clean. Change your water often.

It is best to use spackling or painter's putty to fill the nail holes. Caulk shrinks as it dries, leaving a dimple that will show. Check your spackling or painter's putty directions to see if it says that it is for filling nail holes. Place a small amount of spackling on the center of your putty knife (about the size of a pea) and press this amount into each nail hole.

Decorative Cornices and Shelves

To add even more value and elegance to your home, install decorative crown cornices and shelves. Use the same crown you installed in the room or choose any style you like. These inexpensive cornices and shelves will accent any room and are very simple to build using our compound miter products. If you order ready-made cornices, you could expect to pay about $5 to $7 per inch in length. A standard 40" painted window cornice will cost you around $200 to $300 to have built. If you want wood finish, the price runs even higher. ***You can make the same 40" window cornice for about $15.*** Decorative shelves cost roughly the same because there is very little difference in how the two are made.

In this chapter, I will show you how to build an 80" and two 40" cornices (these dimensions are the inside dimensions from end to end of the cornice). Then, we will cover building a 14' decorative shelf. I will also provide details on how you can adjust the dimensions to get the size you need to build. You will need the Crown Molding Table© or the Miter Table© (if using trim or a miter saw) to obtain the correct settings for your saw. You will also need your True Angle® tools to measure and check all of the corners.

Crown Molding Cornices

Cornice Layout and Dimensions
The first thing to do is decide which type and size of crown you want to use. Get a short sample of the crown and use it to make a full-scale layout of your cornice as shown.

You will need to decide the dimensions of your cornice in order to make your layout. Dimension "A" is the overhang. This can be any size you want. For our example, "A" will be 5/8". Dimension "B" was decided when you chose your crown molding. Dimension "B" is 2-1/8". Dimension "C" is the thickness of the material. In most cases, if you use 1" nominal boards, "C" will be 3/4". You can also use plywood or other materials. Measure the thickness of the material you want to use

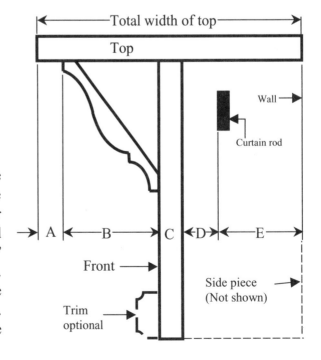

and let that be "C". I will use 1" nominal lumber that is 3/4" thick for this example. Dimension "D" is the distance away from the front of the curtain rod. This normally is 1" to 1-1/2". If you will be using a very full curtain, you may want to make this even larger. We will use 1" for "D". Dimension "E" is measured from the front of the curtain rod to the wall. In this example, "E" is 2-3/4". Make your layout on heavy paper and cut it out. Take your cut-out pattern and hold it up over your curtain to see how it will look and see if you want to change any of the dimensions. The layout for this example has the following dimensions: A=5/8", B=2-1/8", C=3/4", D=1" and E=2-3/4". The lengths of the two curtain rods are 37-7/8" (40" cornice) and 77-7/8" (80" cornice). We will be using these dimensions to calculate the size of the top, front, and sides.

Top Dimensions

To get the width needed for the top of both cornices, add A+B+C+D+E = Total Top Width. For our example, we get 7-1/4". You can also simply measure the full-scale pattern you made. Measure the length of the curtain rod. The length of the top is (A+B+C+D) X 2 + Length of Rod = Total Top Length. In our examples, the curtain rod length is 37-7/8" (for the 40" cornice) and 77-7/8" (for the 80" cornice). A+B+C+D = 4-1/2". Twice that is 9". The total top length for the 40" cornice is 37-7/8"+9" = 46-7/8" and the top length of the 80" cornice is 86-7/8". The dimensions for the top of the cornice are 7-1/4" wide x 3/4" thick x 46-7/8" long (40" cornice) and 86-7/8" long (80" cornice).

Front Dimensions

The width of the front of the cornice is usually the same as the width of the top. You can make this wider or narrower to your preference. The length of the front is 2C+2D+Curtain Rod Length = 41-3/8" long (40" cornice) and 81-3/8" long (80" cornice). The dimensions for the front of the cornice are 7-1/4" wide x 3/4" thick x 41-3/8" long (40" cornice) and 81-3/8" long (80" cornice).

Side Dimensions

The side dimensions are, Length = D+E = 3-3/4". The width is the same as the front width, 7-1/4". You will need two of these -- one for each end.

This table will provide a quick reference for calculating the dimensions of the material needed to build your cornice. Use the dimensions from your cornice layout (see previous page drawing).

Cornice Layout Dimensions		
	Width	Length
Top	A+B+C+D+E	2A+2B+2C+2D+Rod Length
Front	Same as Top	2C+2D+Rod Length
Side (2 ea.)	Same as Front	D+E

I used 3-5/8" wide crown (4" nominal) in this example. We have to cover the two sides and the front with crown. Remember from Chapter 1, to estimate the amount of crown needed, add 1.5 times the width of the crown to each wall length. For our cornice we have three pieces, two wall lengths at 3-3/4" and one wall length at 41-3/8". We will need a piece of crown about 69" long for this cornice. For the optional trim piece, we will need about 69" also.

You are now ready to purchase the material you need to build your cornice. I will be building two window cornices (40") and a double-door cornice (80") for this example. You should purchase grade A pine or top quality knot-free lumber. It will cost a little more, but will look much better when finished.

Cutting the Material

Cut each piece to length using the dimensions we derived. For each cornice, you will have a top, front, and two sides. When cutting out the material, do not forget to account for the saw blade thickness and on which side of the mark to cut. I would suggest you mark and cut one piece at a time.

I used my radial arm saw to cut the material, but you can use any type of saw. Take care and make your cuts square.

I now have all of my cornice boards cut to length.

The next step will be to rip the boards to the proper width of 7-1/4". Make sure your saw blade is set to 90° using your Exact Angle® square. This will make assembly of the cornices much easier. If you prefer, you can rip the boards to the correct width before cutting them to length. If you do not have access to a table saw to rip the boards, you can use a circular saw or adjust dimension "A" so that a standard board width will be the correct width.

Cornice Box Assembly

The first step in assembly is to attach the two sides to the front using clamps. Use wood glue in all joints.

Use three #6 finishing nails (2" long nail for 3/4" material) to attach each side. If you wish to rout the edges with a router, start the nails about 3/4" back from the edge and drive them in at a slight angle. Pre-drill all holes to prevent splitting the wood. Make sure you do not angle the nail too much or it will come through the side of the cornice. If you do not wish to rout your cornice, just center the nails and drive them straight in. You should still pre-drill the holes. Assemble the remaining side in the same manner.

If you are going to rout the edges, you must do so before attaching the top. Choose the router bit you would like to use and make several cuts on a piece of scrap wood. Make any adjustments, then test again on scrap wood. Make sure you secure the wood piece you are working on to prevent it from moving. You will normally rout the front ends, the front and side bottom, and the top upper and lower edges.

The next step will be to attach the top to the front and side assembly. Place a small bead of glue as shown to the front/ side assembly.

Position the top so the back edges are flush and the top is centered over the front/side assembly. There should be a 2-3/4" overhang on each end (A+B). Mark the centerline of the front/side assembly and pre-drill the nail holes. Place two nails in the side and one about every 12" down the front.

Congratulations! You now have all of your basic cornice boxes assembled and are ready to cut and install the crown molding and trim (trim is optional).

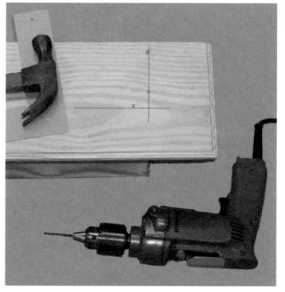

Install the Crown Molding

Let's start by installing the crown to the front of the cornice. Find the left-hand outside corner template that matches the corner we will cut first. You should use your templates for every cut. This will assure the correct cut.

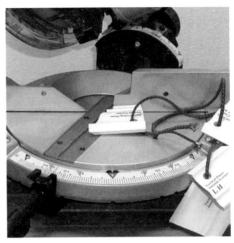

Place the template on your compound miter saw and adjust your saw to fit the template. Use the Original True Angle® to measure the corner angle where you will be installing the crown, and get the correct miter and blade tilt angles from the Crown Molding Table©. Make the final adjustments to your saw.

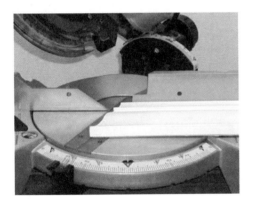

Place the crown molding on your saw exactly like the template was positioned. The bottom of the crown will be against the fence.

If you have a miter saw (blade will not tilt) you can still cut the crown. Just place the template (upside down with the bottom of crown propped against the fence) on your miter saw and adjust the miter to match. Measure the corner angle with the True Angle® and get the miter setting from the Miter Table© (Chapter 3).

Repeat the process of using your templates and setting your saw until all of the crown has been added to your cornice boxes.

Next apply the caulk. Caulk the top, bottom, and joints of the crown molding. (See Chapter 9 for caulking details.)

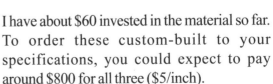

The cornices are ready to paint and install. If you would like to add trim to the bottom of the cornice, do that next.

I have about $60 invested in the material so far. To order these custom-built to your specifications, you could expect to pay around $800 for all three ($5/inch).

Adding Trim

Choose the type trim you would like to add. Your local building supply store should have a wide selection for you to choose from.

Measure the corner angle where the trim will be installed and get the miter setting from the Miter Table©. (See Chapter 3, Baseboards and Trim for more details.)

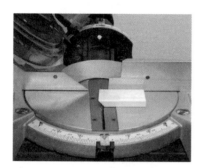

Place your template on your saw and make the necessary adjustments, setting the miter or blade tilt to the angle you obtained from the Miter Table©.

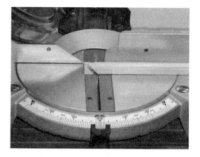

Place your trim on the saw and make the cut. Repeat for the remaining trim pieces. All the cornices are now finished and ready for final caulking and painting.

Hanging the Cornice

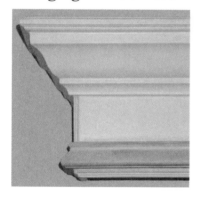

I would recommend using 2-1/2" butt hinges to attach the cornice to the wall. This will allow you to raise the cornice to do any work on the curtain or curtain rod in the future. You will need 1-1/2" wood screws to attach the hinges to the wall because of the drywall thickness.

When installing the hinge to the cornice, notch the back of the cornice to fit the thickness of the hinge. This will allow the cornice to rest fully against the wall. If you use a butt hinge that has a removable pin, you will be able to take the cornice down without having to remove the screws when repainting or working on the cornice. Use two hinges for a window cornice and three hinges for a double-door cornice. For longer cornices, add one hinge for each additional 4' length. Always use a level when mounting the cornices to ensure they are perfectly horizontal. (For additional attachment methods see page 76.)

The cornices are now installed and ready to enjoy. I built these for a fraction of what it would cost to have them custom built. Crown molding shelves are very similar to cornices. We will now cover designing and building a decorative crown molding shelf.

Crown Molding Shelves - (Fireplace mantels are built using the same procedure)

Crown molding shelves are easier to build than cornices. However, the cost of ordering these shelves built to your specifications will cost about the same as a cornice. Crown molding shelves consist of a top, back, and crown molding of your choice.

Crown Shelves Layout and Dimensions

Decide how long and how wide you want the crown shelf. In this example, I will be making a 14' long by 7-1/2" wide shelf for my daughter's room. I will be using 4-5/8" crown molding (5" nominal) with a spring angle of 38°, a 1x8 (3/4" x 7-1/2") for the top and a 1x6 (3/4" x 5-1/2") for the back.

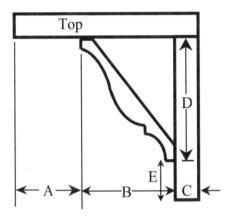

Make a full-scale layout using the crown molding of your choice just as we did for the cornices.

Measure dimension "B" from your layout. For 4-5/8", 38° crown, "B" = 3". A 1x8 (nominal) actually measures 3/4" x 7-1/2". This will give me an overhang dimension for the front of the shelf A = 3-3/4" (A = 7-1/2" - B - C = 3-3/4").

Top Dimensions

You can make your shelf any length and depth you want as long as the shelf is not too small for the crown to fit. My daughter's bedroom is 14' 10" wide. With a 14' shelf, I will have 5" open at each end of the shelf. The top dimensions for this example are 3/4" x 7-1/2" x 14'.

Back Dimensions

To get the length of the back of the shelf, use the overhang dimension you want for the end of the shelf and dimensions "B" and "C" from your layout. I did not want quite as much overhang on the ends as I did in the front, so I chose to make the overhang on each end to be A(end) = 1-1/4". The length of the back needed will be 14'(length of shelf) – (2 X A(end)) – (2 X B) = 14' – 2-1/2" – 6" = 13' 3-1/2".

If using a 1x6, the width of the back will be 5-1/2" (D+E). I also wanted the distance (dimension "E") from the bottom of the crown to the bottom of the back to be the same as the end overhang dimension of 1-1/4". The depth of the crown (dimension "D") is 3-3/4". To get the width, add "D" + "E" = 3-3/4" + 1-1/4" = 5". I will have to rip the back to this width. The back will measure 13' 3-1/2" x 5".

This table will provide a quick reference for calculating the dimensions needed to build your crown shelf. Use the dimensions from your crown shelf layout. The Miter Excel Program® will perform all these calculations for you.

Crown Shelf Layout Dimensions		
	Width	Length
Top	Your choice	Your choice
Back	D+E	Top length – 2XA(end) – 2XB
Crown	N/A	Length of back + 12"

You are now ready to purchase the material you need to build your crown shelf. You should purchase grade A pine or top quality knot-free lumber. It will cost a little more but will look much better when finished.

Cutting the Crown Shelf Material

Cut each piece to length using the dimensions we derived above. For each crown shelf, you will have a top and back. When cutting out the material, do not forget to account for the saw blade thickness and on which side of the mark to cut. I would suggest you mark and cut one piece at a time. I used my radial arm saw to cut out my material, but you can use any type of saw. Take care and make your cuts square.

I now have all of my crown shelf boards cut to the correct length and width and ready to assemble. If you want to rout the edges, you must do this before you assemble the top and back.

Crown Shelf Assembly

Position the top and back as shown, making sure you have the same distance on both ends. I recommend using wood glue in all of the joints. If you do not want to glue the joints, you should use 1-3/4" wood screws. Space the nails/screws about 12" apart. You should pre-drill the holes to prevent splitting the wood.

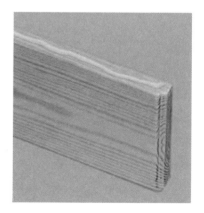

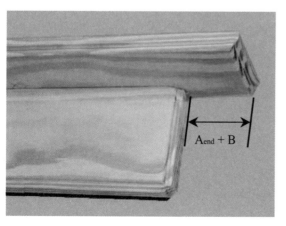

$A_{end} + B$

Congratulations! You now have the crown shelf assembled and are ready to cut and install the crown molding.

Install the Crown Molding

Let's start by installing the crown on the front of the crown shelf. Find the left-hand outside corner template that matches the corner to be cut first. You should use your templates for every cut. This will assure the correct cut.

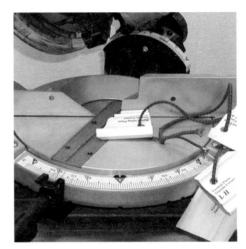

Place the template on your compound miter saw and adjust your saw to fit the template. Use the True Angle® to measure the corner angle where the bottom of the crown will be installed. Obtain the correct miter and blade tilt angles from the Crown Molding Table©, and make the final adjustments to your saw.

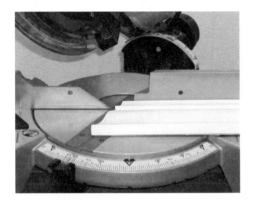

Place the crown molding on your saw exactly like the template was positioned. The bottom of the crown will be against the fence.

If you have a miter saw (blade will not tilt), you can still cut the crown. Just place the template (upside down with the bottom of crown propped against the fence) on your miter saw and adjust the miter to match. Measure the corner angle with the True Angle® and get the miter setting from the Miter Table© (Chapter 3).

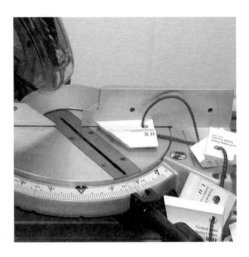

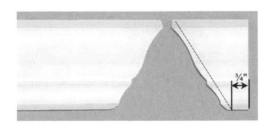

On the right end of the shelf, cut the short return as though you have a 3/4" long wall.

Repeat this for the left end of the crown shelf. Use your templates and the miter and blade tilt angles from the Crown Molding Table© for a compound miter saw or use the Miter Table© for a miter saw. Attach the crown as shown in Chapter 4. You will need to pre-drill any nail holes in the short end pieces.

Caulk the top and bottom of the crown molding (Chapter 9).

The crown shelf is now ready to paint and install.

Installing the Crown Shelf

The crown shelf will usually attach to the wall studs within the wall. Use an electronic wall stud locator and lightly mark the wall studs at the same height as the top of the shelf. Hold the shelf in place and lightly mark the stud locations on the top back of the shelf. Attach the shelf to every third stud (about every 48"). In our example, we will attach the shelf to three wall studs. If your shelf is too short to attach to at least two wall studs, use drywall anchors to attach the shelf. There are several ways to attach your shelf to the wall. I am providing three suggestions, all of which will work equally well. You can find the hardware at your local building/hardware store. Always use a level to ensure that the shelf is horizontal when finished.

Method 1: Attach a metal plate to the top back of the shelf matching the stud locations. Use a minimum of two studs and attach to every third stud. Use at least 1" long #8 or #10 wood screws in the top of the shelf and at least 1-1/2" long #8 or #10 wood screws in the wall studs. Recess the plate 1/8" deep so the shelf/cornice is flush with the wall. A 2" butt hinge may be used instead of the metal plate.

Method 2: Using the marked stud locations on the top of the shelf, insert an eye into the top of the shelf and a hook into the wall. This method will allow you to remove the shelf easily. Attach the shelf to every third wall stud (48" apart).

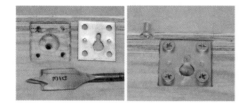

Method 3: If your shelf is mounted below eye level, or if you do not want the attachment brackets to show, you can use this method. Drill a relief hole in the back of the shelf and attach a hidden mount plate as shown. Use a #10 - 2" wood screw in the wall. Leave 3/8" of the screw protruding from the wall. Adjust in or out as necessary to get the shelf to fit snugly against the wall.

The shelf is finished and installed. This 14' long shelf was built for $20.00.

Summary and Review

In this chapter, we covered how to custom-build any size decorative cornice or crown molding shelf/fireplace mantle. The easiest way to do this is to get a sample of the crown you would like to use and make a full-sized layout as described in this chapter.

Cornices

Your layout for a cornice will look very much like this. I have included what are considered to be typical dimensions for a cornice in the table below. You can adjust the dimensions to fit your needs.

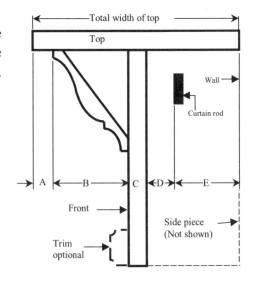

Typical Cornice Dimensions	
A	1/2" to 1"
B	2" to 3-1/2" or more Depends on crown used
C	1/2" to 3/4"
D	1" to 2" or more
E	2-1/2" to 3-1/2" or more Depends on curtain rod used
Front Width	Same as top width

Once you have your dimensions adjusted, you can determine the size of the material with just a few simple calculations using this table.

Cornice Material Dimensions		
Use the dimensions from your layout	Width	Length
Top	A+B+C+D+E	2A+2B+2C+2D+Rod Length
Front	Same as Top	2C+2D+Rod Length
Side (2 ea.)	Same as Front	D+E

If you choose to rout the edges of your cornice, you must do so before attaching the top to the front and side assembly. (Common areas to rout are shown here.)

The crown molding is installed on the corners just as you would cut and install molding on a 270° outside corner. The end of the crown molding will have a square cut that fits against the wall.

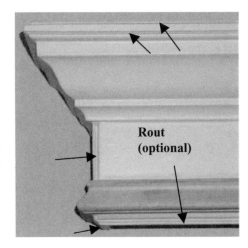

http://www.compoundmiter.com, a Quint Group company, since March 2000

Crown Shelves/Fireplace Mantles

Make a full-sized layout of your crown shelf using the crown of your choice.

When you have the dimensions to your liking, use the table below to cut your material.

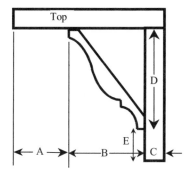

Crown Shelf Material Dimensions		
	Width	Length
Top	Your choice	Your choice
Back	D+E	Top length – 2Aend – 2B
Crown	N/A	Length of back + 12"

If you rout the crown shelf, you must do so before you attach the top to the back.

Return the crown molding to the wall on both ends for a beautiful shelf that will complement any decor. Returning the crown is just like turning an outside corner. This is also the method used to end crown in the middle of a wall (Chapter 8).

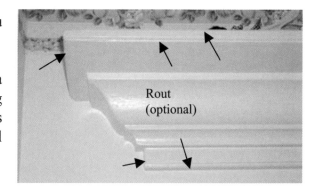

Rout (optional)

Cornices and crown shelves/fireplace mantles add beauty and elegance to any room. They can be built for a fraction of the cost of ordering them custom-built to your specifications. Even a novice can build one. All you need are the right tools and information.

Coping

In this chapter, I will deal with how to properly cope a joint. We will first cover techniques for trim that is placed flat on the wall. The types of trim include baseboards, chair rails, quarter and half-round trim, cove molding, corner molding, fireplace trim, and door and window casings. Then, I will provide you with some techniques for coping crown molding.

Coping is simply transferring the contour of one piece of trim (or crown molding) to a second piece of trim, then cutting along the contour line with a coping saw so that, when finished, the second piece of trim will mate to the first piece with minimal gaps. Any small voids remaining are then caulked and painted.

You will need a coping saw and a scribe. (See photo to the right). The coping saw ($5 to $8) and the scribe ($1 to $2) can both be purchased at your local building supply store.

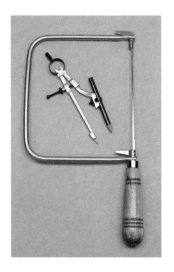

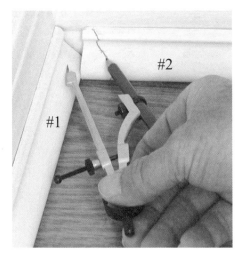

Coping Trim
The simplest corners to cope are inside corners that measure 90° ± 5°.

To cope an inside corner, nail the first piece of trim (#1, square cut) in place all the way into the corner, then butt the second piece (#2) of trim up to it. (See photo to the left.)

Take your scribe and let the sharp, pointed end rest against trim piece #1 (the square cut piece). While holding your scribe horizontally, move it up and down to create a profile contour on the second piece of trim. Use both hands on the scribe to steady it and concentrate on holding it horizontally. This will help get a more accurate contour transfer.

After you have the profile transferred, take your coping saw and carefully cut along the profile line. (See photo to the right). **Note:** You should undercut the piece of trim about 5°. For example, if you are coping trim to fit a 90° corner, cut the trim about 95° as shown. You can use your True Angle® to assist in lining up your saw to make the 5° undercut.

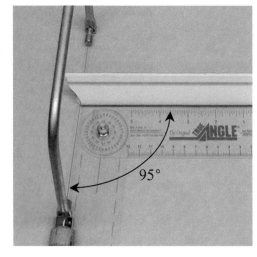

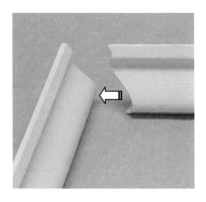

Check-fit the trim to see if you need to sand (or file) for a better fit. If you are going to caulk and paint the trim, do not worry too much about getting a perfect fit.

If you are installing stain-grade (wood finish) trim, you will need to make the fit as close as possible and will need to use sand paper or a file to get a perfect fit.

Another technique to transfer a contour for trim is to use a contour gauge (around $5 to $8). A contour gauge consists of many small diameter steel rods that are clamped snugly in the middle but will slide when pushed on the end. (This only works well for trim that is placed flat on the wall. This technique *will not* work well for crown molding.)

Gently press down on the contour gauge until the matching contour shape has formed on the other side. (See photo to the left.)

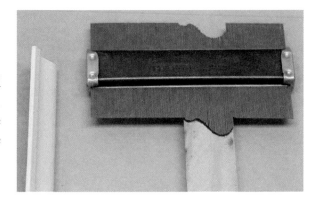

Then, take your contour gauge and place the formed contour on the back of the trim that you wish to cope. Make sure the top of the contour matches the top of the trim, then draw the contour on the back of the trim to be coped.

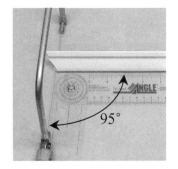

You will use your coping saw as you did before, except now you will be coping along the contour placed on the back of the trim instead of the front.

When you have installed your trim, a light application of caulk will be necessary. Then your trim should be touched up with paint (see Chapter 9 on caulking).

Coping Crown Molding

To cope crown molding, you will need a coping saw and a scribe as previously illustrated for coping trim.

Extend the first piece of crown molding (square cut end) into the corner and nail in place. Make sure that both pieces of crown molding are at the *correct installed angle*. (The bottom of the crown should be held firmly against the wall while letting the top rest on the ceiling naturally. See Chapter 4 for tips on aligning and installing the crown.) You can nail the first piece (#1) of crown molding in place at this point. You will then hold the second piece (#2) of crown molding next to the first, as shown in the photo to the right. Take your scribe and draw a contour of the first piece of crown molding onto the second piece. You must hold the scribe horizontally while moving it up and down in order to get an accurate contour transfer.

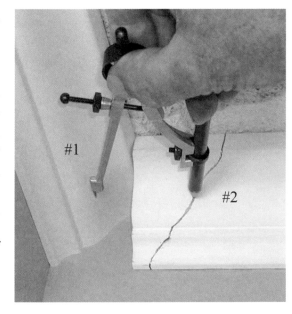

To cope the second piece of crown molding, you will need to place the crown upside down and propped up so that when you saw, you will be able to undercut the crown about 5° as we did above with trim. Again use your True Angle® as a guide and set it on the corner angle plus 5°. For a 90° corner, you would cut the crown at 95°, as shown in the photo to the right. Carefully cut along the contour line while holding your coping saw horizontally.

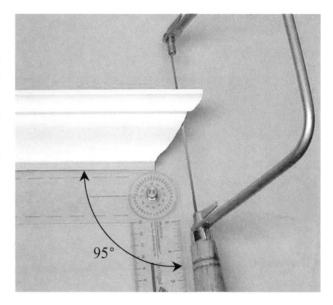

When you have the second piece of crown molding trimmed to your satisfaction, it is ready to install. Remember, if you are caulking and painting your trim, a few small voids will not make any difference. However, natural-wood finish trim will require a considerable amount of hand-fitting to get the perfect mating joint.

The contour gauge used for trim above is just too difficult to use for crown molding. The crown slope and the irregular surfaces of the crown make it impractical.

Summary and Review

To properly cope a joint (trim or crown molding), you will need a scribe and a coping saw. The scribe is used to transfer the contour of the surface of one piece of trim to another. When you cut along the transferred contour line, the two pieces of trim will fit together to form a mating joint. Because of the difficulty of getting a perfect fit, coping is usually reserved for paint-grade crown or trim where you will be caulking and painting.

I am frequently asked, "Isn't a coped joint better than a mitered joint and much less likely to separate over time?" NO! Some people have the misconceived notion that a coped joint is much better than a mitered joint and less likely to separate over time. That is simply not true. All wood tends to absorb and expel moisture. This causes the wood to expand and contract as the moisture content varies. Today's millwork material is kiln-dried before it is manufactured and is much more stable than wood products used in the early days of construction.

During installation, a miter joint is more likely to separate in the joint if you drive your nails too close to the end. A coped joint will also move, but the movement is not quite as noticeable due to the way the joint is mated. To minimize movement during installation (either coping or mitering), position the crown or trim firmly in place while nailing and, if possible, do not nail any closer than 6" to 8" from the corner.

You can achieve a beautiful looking crown or trim job by coping your joints, but it is very time consuming and difficult, especially for the novice. If you have more that just a few corners, I would recommend that you use another method to cut your joints.

Miter Boxes

There are several types of miter boxes available. In this chapter, we will cover how to use miter boxes, as well as some of their advantages and disadvantages. The three types shown below can be purchased at almost any building supply store.

One of the most attractive features of these miter boxes is the price. Both the 12" wood miter box and the 12" yellow plastic miter box (plastic miter box to the left in the photo) sell for around $5. These two miter boxes do not come with a saw. If you already have a handsaw, it should work, provided it is long enough to reach through the miter box and still have enough length for sawing. (For these miter boxes, you will need at least a 14" handsaw.)

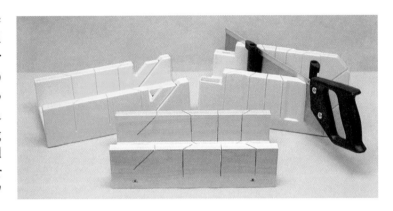

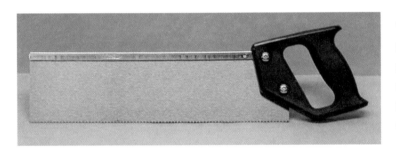

This is a 14" backsaw that is recommended for cutting crown molding and trim using a miter box. However, if you are cutting large crown molding, you may need to resort to a regular handsaw. (I will cover this in more detail later in this chapter.)

The third type of miter box that we will address is a clamping miter box with saw, as shown in the upper right photo. This unit sells for about $15 and includes the backsaw. The cam pins come in very handy. They will help hold your work piece and provide assistance in properly aligning your crown molding at the correct angle while cutting.

Cutting Templates Using a Miter Box
Before we begin our discussion of miter boxes, I would like to illustrate how to cut a set of templates for yourself using a miter box. It does not matter which of these miter boxes you use, the templates will all be cut the same. I will use the wood miter box for my illustrations.

Templates for Trim Applications

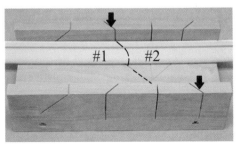

I have placed my trim standing up with the bottom of the trim on the base of the miter box (see photo to the left). I inserted my saw into the 45° vertical slots indicated by the arrows. Trim piece #1 is a horizontal turn, outside 270° corner, left-hand piece. Trim piece #2 is a horizontal turn, inside 90° corner, right-hand piece. Cut these about 3" long and label them. For example, write on trim piece #1, "horizontal turn, outside 90° corner, left-hand piece". Label all of your templates in the same manner.

For the next piece, notice the changes that I have made. The trim is in the exact same position, standing upright against the back of the miter box, and I have used the opposite set of 45° vertical slots. Trim piece #3 is a horizontal turn, inside 90° corner, left-hand piece. Trim piece #4 is a horizontal turn, outside 270° corner, right-hand piece. Cut these about 3" long and label each. (See photo to the right.)

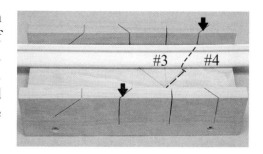

The remaining trim templates are for cutting trim that turns upward or downward in a vertical plane (the wall). You will need these if you are installing trim on wainscoting, along a stairway, or simply making a picture frame.

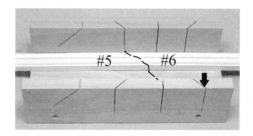

Place your trim laying flat in your miter box with the bottom of the trim towards you. Trim piece #5 is a vertical turn, inside 90° corner, left-hand piece. Trim piece #6 is a downward turn, 270° outside corner, right-hand piece. (See photo to the left.)

To cut the last two trim templates, I have moved my saw to the other set of 45° vertical slots. Trim piece #7 is a downward turn, 270° outside corner, left-hand piece. Trim piece #8 is an upward turn, 90° inside corner, right-hand piece. (See photo to the right.)

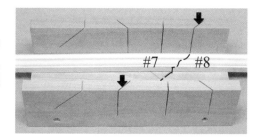

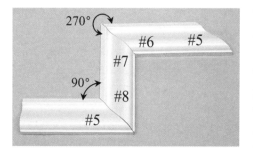

The vertical plane templates for trim are a little more difficult to describe, so I have provided an example of each (see photo to the left). You can see (working from left to right) that if you have a trim piece #5 cut, then you will need to cut a trim piece #8 to fit next to it. The same applies to #7 and #6. At the open piece #5, which trim cut would you make to join it? (Answer: #8). If, instead of cutting the last trim cut as a #5, which would you cut to turn the trim downward? (Answer: #7 and then a #6 to join it). By the way, to make the above eight trim cuts, the 45° slanted slot would work just as well.

Once again, it will save you a lot of frustration if you make yourself a set of templates and use them as a guide. The templates will show you how to position your material to get the correct cut.

Templates for Crown Molding Applications

I will now show you how to make your eight templates for crown molding using your miter box. You should cut them about 3" long and write the description on each template as we did with the trim templates. (These templates are identical to the templates described in Chapters 3, 4 and 5.)

For horizontal turns of crown molding using a miter box, always place the crown molding upside down with the bottom of the crown held firmly against the back of the miter box.

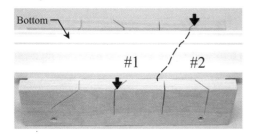

Crown molding template #1 is a horizontal turn, inside 90° corner, right-hand piece. Crown molding piece #2 is a horizontal turn, outside 270° corner, left-hand piece. The arrows indicate which slots to insert your saw to cut your crown templates.

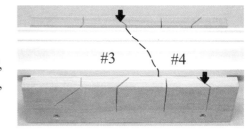

Crown molding template #3 is a horizontal turn, outside 270° corner, right-hand piece. Crown molding template #4 is a horizontal turn, inside 90° corner, left-hand piece.

Your set of templates for horizontal turns should look like the templates in the photo to the right. Drill a 3/8" hole in each template in order to bundle them together. Use a small diameter rope and keep them with your miter box.

We will next cover the templates needed for making upward or downward turns with crown molding. When using a miter box for these, you will only be able to make 90° turns. If you have a cathedral/vaulted ceiling, you will not be able to use any of these miter boxes in this chapter to cut your crown. However, the miter box will work fine for applications like placing crown along a staircase where you would be making 90° turns only.

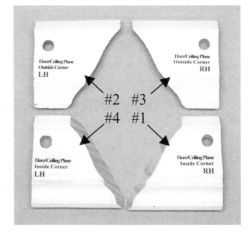

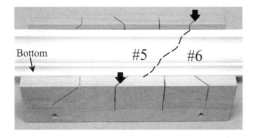

For vertical turns (upward/downward) of crown molding, you will place your crown in your miter box with the bottom of the crown held firmly against the bottom of your miter box. (See photo to the right.) Crown molding template #5 is a vertical turn (downward), inside 90° corner, left-hand piece. Crown molding template #6 is a vertical turn (upward), outside 270° corner, right-hand piece.

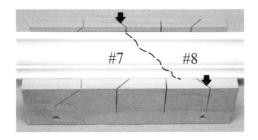

For the last two crown molding templates for vertical turns, you will use the opposite set of 45° vertical slots.

Crown molding template #7 is a vertical turn (upward), outside 270° corner, left-hand piece. Crown molding template #8 is a vertical turn (downward), inside 90° corner, right-hand piece.

Your set of vertical turn templates should look like the set in the picture to the right.

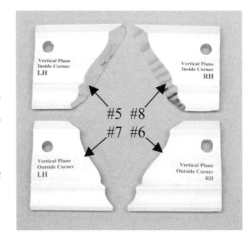

Wood Miter Box -12"

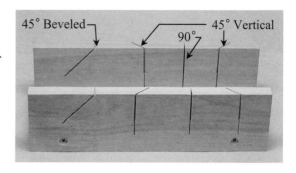

The 12" wood miter box has left and right 45° vertical slots, a 90° square cut slot, and a 45° beveled slot. The type of corner cuts that you can make with a miter box are limited to inside 90° and outside 270° corners and square cuts. A miter box is best suited for rooms that are rectangular. You are also limited to cutting the smaller sizes of crown molding (2-3/4" wide) and trim (3-3/4" wide).

From the photo to the right, you can see that the front of this miter box is wider than the back and extends below the base. This allows you to place the miter box on the edge of a table to help hold the miter box while sawing. You can also drill some mounting holes through the base and secure the miter box with screws.

Trim

I have provided detailed instructions for cutting trim with a miter saw in Chapter 3. Please review that chapter. If you are a novice and have trouble visualizing how to place your trim in your miter box to get the correct corner cut, make and label a set of templates for yourself as described earlier in this chapter under "Cutting Templates Using a Miter Box".

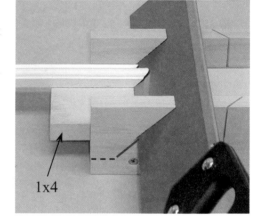

There is usually more than one way to position your trim to get the same corner cut. When we made our templates for trim (see trim template #1), we had the trim standing vertically and used the 45° vertical slots. You can also position your trim flat, as shown in the photo to the right, to cut an outside 270° corner, left-hand piece. Notice that the bottom of the base cap that I am cutting is positioned towards me and the top is next to the back of the miter box.

Most new wood miter boxes do not have the slots cut all the way to the base. The vertical slots can be extended to the base with no problem, but I would not advise doing so with the 45° beveled slot. If you cut the 45° beveled slot all the way to the bottom of the miter box, it will weaken the wood that holds the corner intact and will be much easier to break along the dashed line (see above photo). To use the 45° beveled slot, it is best to place a 1x4 in the bottom of the wood miter box to raise the trim.

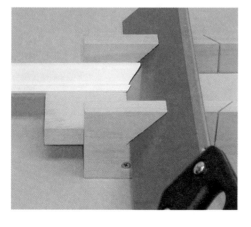

Trim (baseboards, chair rails, etc.) can be cut either standing up against the back of the miter box or laying flat as shown. This miter box is 2-3/16" deep. If your trim is wider than that, you will need to lay the trim flat to cut it. Most baseboard trim is 3-1/4" wide or wider. By laying your trim flat and using the 45° bevel slots, you can cut trim up to the width of the inside of the miter box (3-3/4" for this miter box). It is also much easier to hold the trim while sawing.

This is the opposite mating cut which is an outside 270° corner, right-hand piece (see photo to the left). The top of the trim is now towards me.

To cut an inside 90° corner, you will simply place the trim on the opposite side of the saw (right-hand side) and cut as shown in the previous two photos for a 90° outside corner. (Use your trim templates while working to prevent cutting the trim backwards.)

When you need to butt your trim up to a door jam or any place that you need to make a square cut, you will position the trim as shown and use the 90° vertical slots.

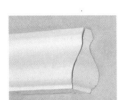

There may be times when you might want to end the trim without butting it against a door jam. For that, you can cut what is called a return. This is simply an outside 270° corner with the right-hand piece cut square and butted into the wall. This also applies to crown molding (see Chapter 8).

Crown Molding

Cutting crown molding using a miter box is the same as shown in Chapter 4. The crown molding shown here is 2-3/4" wide. This is the largest size you can cut with this miter box. Any larger and the crown will be above the saw guides.

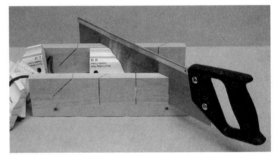

Place your template as shown for the type of cut that you need. This is an outside 270° corner, right-hand piece. Make sure that the crown is placed **upside down** for all horizontal turns with the bottom of the crown held firmly against the back of the miter box. (The top of crown is often milled at a 3° relief angle and should not be used for positioning the crown molding.)

Below are the remaining cuts for horizontal crown molding.

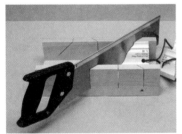

Outside 270° corner
left-hand piece.

Inside 90° corner
left-hand piece.

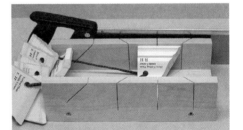

Inside 90° corner
right-hand piece.

As you can see from the pictures above, using your set of templates will allow you to determine exactly how to place your crown in your miter box and to cut it correctly every time.

If the crown molding you want to install is too large for the miter box, as shown here, you can add extensions to your miter box.

You will also need to cut the saw slots and add an extension to the front of the miter box. (Shown here is 4" crown molding.)

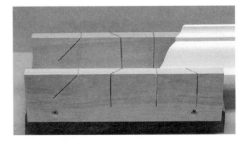

http://www.compoundmiter.com, a Quint Group company, since March 2000

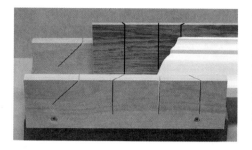

To modify your miter box, add extensions to the front and back of the miter box (back extension shown). If you are using a backsaw, your extensions cannot exceed the width of the backsaw blade or you will not be able to cut all the way through your crown molding or trim. As an alternative, you can use a regular handsaw that does not have the stiffener down the top of the blade.

Before you go to this effort of adding extensions, you might consider building you own miter box. I have included some guidelines and tips on how to build your own at the end of this chapter.

Yellow Plastic Miter Box - 12"

This plastic miter box is identical to the wood miter box above and costs about the same ($5, saw not included). The depth and the inside width are the same, so you can cut the same size trim and crown molding.

The front of the plastic miter box is also made to sit on the edge of any stationary object to hold it steady while cutting, and it has mounting holes.

One advantage plastic boxes have over the wood boxes is that they are much more durable and less likely to break if dropped.

Trim

You will place your trim in the plastic box the same way you would in the wood miter box above. (Use your templates as a guide). This is an outside 270° corner, left-hand piece. For the plastic miter box, it is not necessary to place a 1x4 in the bottom to raise the trim.

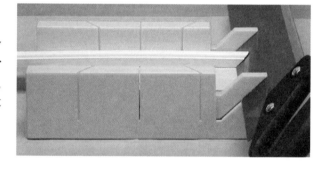

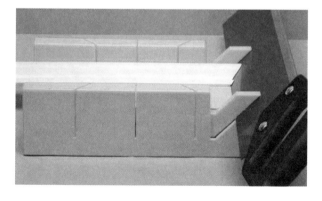

I have placed my base cap trim for the opposite cut in this photo to the left. This is an outside 270° corner, right-hand piece.

Crown Molding

You will also cut your crown molding the same as with the wood miter box above. Position the template for the corner you want to cut, then position your crown molding in exactly the same position and make the cut. This is an outside 270° corner, right-hand piece.

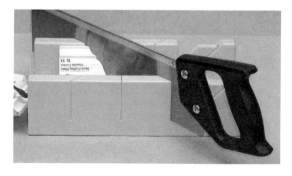

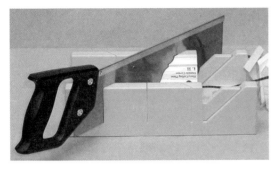

Use your set of templates to position your crown molding for the remaining corner cuts that you need. This is an outside 270° corner, left-hand piece.

You can also purchase a set of crown molding templates through our web site.

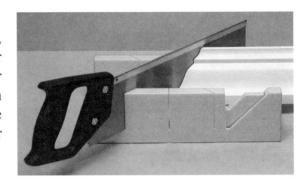

If you want to install crown molding larger than 2-3/4", you will have the same problem as with the wood miter box above. This crown molding is too large for the miter box. You will either need to modify the miter box with front and back extensions or make a miter box. (See the example at the end of this chapter on how to build a miter box.)

Clamping Miter Box

The clamping miter box is the most versatile of these three miter boxes. The miter box is 3" deep and 4-3/4" wide. It will accommodate larger crown molding and trim. This miter box also has 22.5° right and left vertical slots. The 22.5° slots (see arrows) will allow cutting those corner angles that are for a 135° inside or a 225° outside corner. You will run into this corner angle often when dealing with a bay window or other corners where the wall makes a 45° turn.

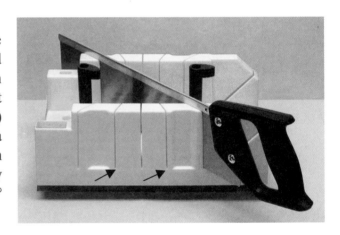

Like the previous miter boxes, the clamping miter box has the extension on the front that allows you to place the miter box on the edge of a table, and has mounting holes molded into the base.

I especially like the cam locking pins. With these, you will be able to secure your trim (standing up or placed flat) while cutting. If your pins are a little loose, wrap one to two layers of scotch tape around the peg that goes in the base. The scotch tape will usually fix the problem.

Trim

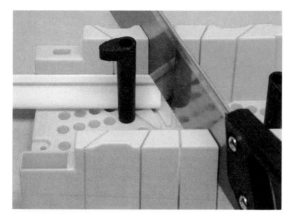

Here, I have some base cap trim securely clamped, and I am cutting a 225° outside corner, left-hand piece. Remember, as long as the trim does not extend beyond the top of the miter box, you can cut it standing vertically. If your trim extends beyond the top of your miter box, you will need to lay the trim flat to cut it. The 45° slanted slot in this miter box is for 90° or 270° corners, so you would not be able to cut a 225° corner with your trim placed flat.

Note: Do not twist the cam locks too tightly or you will dent your trim.

Crown Molding

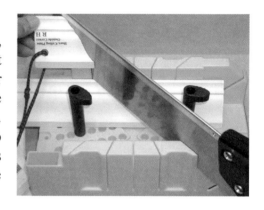

When you use your clamping miter box for cutting crown molding, you will be able to adjust the cam clamps so that when you insert your crown it will be held at the correct angle for cutting. For horizontal turns, place your crown molding upside down with the bottom of the crown held firmly against the back of the miter box. The cam pins need to be wedged against an object in order to become tight. When cutting crown, they are used only as stops and can be loose. The scotch tape mentioned before will solve the problem.

For the remaining horizontal crown molding cuts, use your crown molding templates as a guide to position your crown for cutting. You can also cut your crown molding for vertical turns. For a vertical turn, you will need to position the crown with the bottom resting firmly on the base of the miter box. Again, use you crown molding templates as a guide.

Note: After you cut your crown molding or trim, if you find that the corners do not come together to suit your taste, you can file the heel of the crown or trim to make it fit better. This occurs when the corner on which you are installing your crown molding or trim is not a true 90° corner. If, for example, the corner is actually 93° and you used a miter box, you will have a small gap in the joint. Use sandpaper, a wood rasp or other tools to remove the interference from the joint to make it fit better. As long as you are using paint-grade material, almost all of the gaps can be caulked and painted for excellent results, even without sanding.

Build Your Own Miter Box

If you would like to install crown molding or trim that is too large for these miter boxes, you might consider building your own miter box. For much less than the cost of purchasing a more expensive electric or hand-operated miter saw, you can easily build one to suit your own needs.

By definition, a **miter** is the joint formed by two pieces of molding, each cut at an angle so they can completely butt against each other when joined to form a corner. The easiest way to determine the miter angle (also know as the **face angle**) for your miter box is to measure the corner angle with your True Angle® and divide by 2. For example, if your corner measured 135°, the miter angle/face angle would be 67.5° (135°/2 = 67.5°). We will use this definition —*face angle*— to lay out the slots that we will cut in our miter box.

Note: Do not get this miter angle/face angle mixed up with the miter angles that I have in all of the charts and tables in this book. The charts and tables in this book all show the complement of the face angle, e.g., 90° minus the face angle. I have set up the charts and tables to accommodate the scales of most miter saws which use the complement of the face angle. Some saws display both scales.

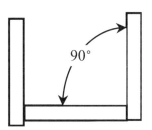

To build a miter box that will accommodate up to 8" crown molding or 7-1/2" wide trim, you will need both a 1x8 that is 8' long and a standard handsaw. (If you would like to make a heavier duty miter box, cut the base from a 2x8 and the front and back from a 2x10 and use 3" screws.) Cut the 8' board into three 32" lengths and assemble as shown in the end view drawing of the miter box to the right. Let the front of the miter box extend below the base 3/8" to 1/2". Use grade A quality lumber (knot-free), #10 or #12 1-1/2" long wood screws (4 on each side), and glue the joints. Make sure the front and back are square with the base.

After you have your miter box assembled, you will need to saw your slots using a regular handsaw. You will need to take care in sawing these to make sure they are correct.

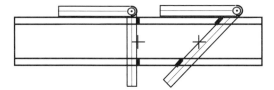

Use your 18" True Angle® to lay out a 90° square cut (midway as shown to the right). To lay out your first 45° slots, set your True Angle® on 45° and mark as shown. You should center the 45° set of slots 1/4 the length of the miter box from the end.

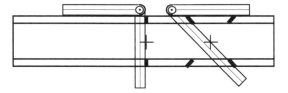

Then flip your True Angle® over while still set on 45°, and make your next set of marks (see drawing to the left).

Note: The slots must be cut vertically. Use your True Angle® set at 90° and draw a saw line that extends from your top marks all the way down to the base of the miter box. You can do this on the inside or outside (whichever you prefer), but you must saw on these lines. Do not cut your slots too close together or the narrow wood pieces could easily break.

The saw slots we have just added will allow you to cut all of your crown molding and trim for rectangular rooms. If you have any corners that are not 90° ± 5°, you can use the other half of your new miter box to cut slots that will match the corners you need. If you have trim (baseboards) wider than 6-3/4", you may want to cut a 45° bevel (slanted) slot. You can then lay your trim flat and cut up to 7-1/2" wide trim. It is best not to cut the slanted slot all the way to the bottom of your miter box (see 12" wood miter box).

For corners other than 90°, you will need to add additional slots. For example, let's say that you have a bay window where the wall makes a 45° turn (135° inside and 225° outside corner) and you would like to install your crown molding or trim around the bay window. To cut these new slots for the bay window, measure the corner angle and divide by 2. You will cut these as you did before making sure the slots are vertical.

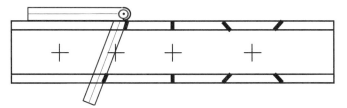

The 135° inside corner divided by 2 will equal 67.5°. Set your True Angle® on 67.5° and mark your miter box as shown in the drawing to the left.

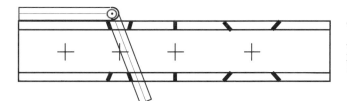

The 225° corner divided by 2 will equal 112.5°. Set your True Angle® on 112.5°, and mark your miter box as shown in the drawing to the left.

You will now be able to cut your crown molding or trim for your bay window using these new slots. You still have room for additional slots if you have other corners that do not match the existing slots that you have. Just remember, to add slots to your miter box, measure the corner angle and divide by 2. Then mark the slots on the top of your miter box as shown and cut them vertically.

Summary and Review

The miter boxes that I have covered in this chapter will provide excellent results and are very inexpensive when compared to purchasing a powered miter or compound miter saw. These miter boxes are very well suited for up to 3" crown molding or trim installed in rectangular (90° corners) rooms.

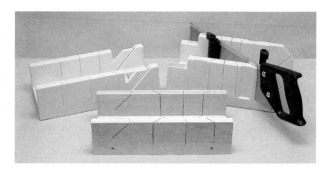

The advantage of these miter boxes is obviously the cost. They are without a doubt the least expensive tool needed to cut your crown molding or trim. However, they do have disadvantages. For example, miter boxes are limited to smaller crown molding or trim applications and also to 90° corners. But if you have only rectangular rooms, any of these will allow you to easily cut and install crown molding or trim throughout your entire home.

I have also included information to help you build your own miter box if these manufactured miter boxes are too small for your crown molding or trim, and you do not want to invest in the more expensive miter or compound miter saws. You will still be limited to 90° corners and a few odd-angled corners that you may have, but you will be able to cut up to 8" crown molding or 7 1/2" trim.

I would not recommend using a miter box for cathedral ceilings. You will need much more adjustment capability and should use at least an adjustable miter saw — either electric or manual. If you do not want to purchase an electric miter or compound miter saw, tool rental yards have them available.

Adjustable Miter Boxes

An interim step between the previously-mentioned fixed miter boxes (Chapter 12) and the adjustable, electric miter and compound miter saws (Chapters 3, 4, and 5) is the adjustable steel miter box that comes with an attached saw. I will cover two types that are available and how to use them.

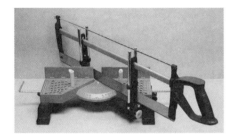

Protractor Miter Box

This clamping protractor miter box has an adjustable miter setting. With this miter adjustment, you will be able to cut any crown molding or trim for any application, provided the crown or trim is not too large for the saw. To use the saw, the crown molding will need to be propped up against the fence. This adjustable miter box saw sells for about $40.

The second type of saw we will cover is a hand compound miter saw that has both miter and blade tilt adjustments. This type of saw will allow you to cut your crown molding and trim placed flat on the saw table. This saw also comes with hold-down clamps, plus a few other useful adjustable devices for positioning and holding your work piece. This sells for about $70.

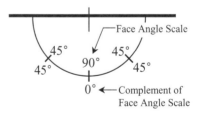

Compound Miter Box

You will need to make a full set of templates to use with either of the saws. To cut your templates using a protractor miter box, follow the instructions for an electric **miter** saw as shown in Chapters 3, 4, and 5. To cut your templates using a compound miter box, follow the instructions for an electric **compound miter** saw, also shown in Chapters 3, 4, and 5. Your set of templates will prevent you from getting confused and cutting your trim or crown molding backwards.

Why would anyone get *confused* cutting their crown molding or trim? Look at it this way. There are 4 joints for crown molding (8 templates) and 4 joints for trim (8 templates). For a compound miter saw that has blade tilt in both directions there are two ways to cut each template. That means you could have at least 32 combinations to cut your crown molding and trim. No wonder the novice can get confused! Make it easy on yourself. Make a set of templates and use them.

Note About Face Angle: I have adopted the most commonly used reference for a miter angle = 0° as a square cut (complement of the face angle). It is used throughout this book in all the charts and tables. However, some saws will show a miter setting of 90° as being a square cut (the scale is reversed — see drawing to the right). This 90° square cut angle is commonly referred to as the *face angle* and is the angle measured from the fence to the saw blade. Both of the saws in this chapter have the *face angle* as the miter scale (90° is a square cut). Check your adjustable miter box to see which scale you have. If your saw uses the *face angle* as the miter scale, you will need to subtract the miter setting found in the tables and charts in this book from 90° in order to get the face angle.

Saw Top View

Protractor Miter Box

Let's begin our detailed discussion with the adjustable protractor miter box. You will use this saw exactly like the power miter saw detailed in Chapters 3, 4, and 5. All of your crown molding and trim will be placed on your saw the same way. For example, crown molding that will be making horizontal turns will be placed on your protractor miter box upside down and backwards. For upward or downward turns, place the bottom of the crown firmly on the saw table (same as in Chapter 5).

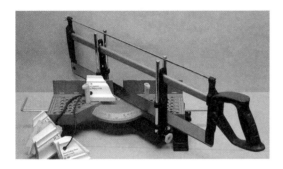

To use an adjustable miter box that has a 0° miter as a square cut (complement of the face angle), measure the corner angle with your True Angle® and look up the miter setting in the Miter Table© (Chapter 3). Use the template for the corner you wish to cut as a guide. Here, I have placed my template for a horizontal turn, outside corner, right-hand piece on my saw and have set the miter to the correct setting. Position your crown to match your template, and make the cut.

If your protractor miter box has the face angle miter scale (90° is a square cut), subtract the miter setting found in Miter Table© from 90° to get the face angle. For inside corners, you can obtain the face angle by measuring the corner angle with the True Angle® and dividing by 2. For outside corners, subtract the measured corner angle from 360°, then divide by 2. For example, if your corner angle measures 135° (inside corner) and your saw has the **face angle** scale, you would set your miter on 67.5° (135° ÷ 2 = 67.5°). If you have a 225° corner (outside corner), you would still set you saw on 67.5° (360°-225° = 135°, then divide by 2 = 67.5°).

Here are more examples of how to position your crown molding. The photo to the left is an upward turn, outside corner, left-hand piece.

The photo to the right is for an upward turn, outside corner, right-hand piece.

Upward and downward turns are needed while installing crown on a cathedral ceiling. Hold the bottom of the crown firmly on the saw table.

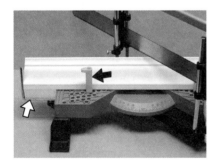

This saw has two other nice features. The adjustable stop (white arrow) fits on either side of the saw, and is used when cutting several pieces the same size, such as when installing trim on wainscoting or a staircase. The clamping pegs (black arrow) help hold your work piece in place.

This adjustable protractor miter box has a very short back fence to rest your crown against. If you are installing 3" crown molding, you can let your crown rest just on the top of the fence, as shown in the end-

view drawing to the right. However, you must make sure that the bottom of the crown is vertical, as though it were actually resting *against* the fence while placed upside down. Use the clamping pegs to help position your crown.

If you want to install crown molding larger than 3", you will need to add a fence extension to both sides of your saw. Cut both of your fence extensions 5" tall, as shown in the drawing to the right. Install one fence extension on each side of your saw blade, 90° to the saw table. Drill a couple of holes through each fence, then use #10 or #12 countersunk bolts and nuts to attach them.

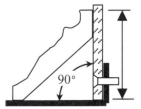

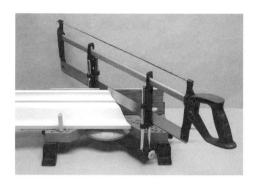

In this photo, I have attached my fence extensions and now can easily cut up to 5" crown molding using my protractor miter box. Positioning the crown is now much easier, especially with the assistance of the clamping pegs.

6" crown is the largest that this saw will cut. Your particular saw may handle larger crown, but not much larger. Beyond 6" size, you will need to resort to a larger saw, preferably a sliding compound miter saw so you will be able to lay your crown molding flat.

The fence extensions shown here were cut from scrap pieces of hardwood flooring. You can also use 3/8" to 1/2" plywood. Make sure that your extensions, when installed, are square (90°) with the table of your saw. With the fence extensions, your adjustable miter box will be able to handle baseboards that need to be cut standing up. Use your templates as a guide for positioning your crown molding or trim on your saw.

Compound Miter Box

This compound miter box has both miter and blade tilt adjustment and is the most versatile of all the adjustable miter boxes. You will place all of your crown molding or trim laying flat and face up on the saw table.

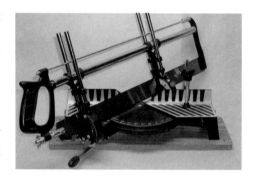

As mentioned earlier in this chapter, the miter scale on some saws is reversed and uses the *face angle* (90° as a square cut). If your saw displays the *face angle* as the miter scale, you must subtract the miter settings, obtained from the charts and tables from 90° to get the face angle (e.g., 90°- miter setting = *face angle*).

I have placed my template for a horizontal turn, outside corner, left-hand piece on my saw. Using my template, for this cut I know to rotate my miter setting clockwise and tilt the saw blade to the left. The saw blade for this compound miter box will tilt in both directions, to the right and to the left. I could have just as easily placed the same template with the top of the crown molding against the fence and on the left side of the saw blade. In that case, I would have rotated my miter counter-clockwise, tilted my saw blade to the right, and made the same cut.

For a **compound miter box** that uses the *face angle* scale (90° is a square cut), measure the corner angle with the True Angle®, obtain the miter angle from the appropriate chart or table in this book, then subtract it from 90° to get the face angle. For example, if you are installing 38° spring angle crown and want to make a horizontal turn, 135° inside corner (from the Crown Molding Table©), the miter angle = 14.3° and the blade tilt angle = 17.6°. The *face angle* would be 90° - 14.3° = 75.7°. You would then set your saw on 75.7° and the blade tilt = 17.6°. **Note:** A vertical blade is *always* referenced as a 0° blade tilt (square cut) for all saws.

Summary and Review

I have covered two types of adjustable miter box saws in this chapter.

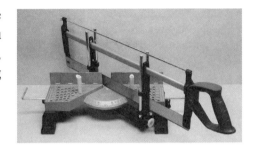

The first was an adjustable protractor miter box. This saw will be used exactly like the electric miter saw in Chapters 3, 4, and 5. You will place your template on your saw, make the adjustments to match, then set your saw using the charts and tables that apply (depending on your saw's miter scale).

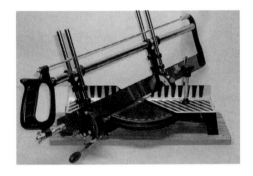

The second type of saw is a compound miter box with both miter and blade tilt adjustment. This is the most versatile of all the adjustable miter boxes. You will place all of your crown molding and trim laying flat on the saw table, then use the miter and/or blade tilt setting found in the charts and tables that apply (depending on your saw's miter scale).

There are two different miter scales used. On one miter scale, a miter setting of 0° will give you a square cut (complement of the face angle scale). The other scale uses a miter setting of 90° to give you a square cut (face angle scale).

Throughout this book, I have used the most commonly recognized scale where a miter angle = 0° as a square cut (complement of the face angle). However, both of the saws illustrated in this chapter have a miter setting of 90° as being a square cut (face angle scale) where the miter scale is reversed. This 90° square cut angle is referred to as the *face angle*. If this is the case with your saw, you will need to subtract the miter setting obtained from the Miter Table©, the Crown Molding Table©, or the Compound Miter Chart© from 90° to get your *face angle* setting.

For a **protractor miter box** that uses a 90° setting as a square cut, to get the *face angle* you can (1) Measure the corner angle, look up the miter setting in the Miter Table© and subtract it from 90°, *OR* (2) For inside corners, measure the corner angle and divide by 2; for outside corners, measure the corner angle, subtract it from 360 and divide by 2.

For a **compound miter box** that uses a 90° setting as a square cut, to get the face angle you need to measure the corner angle, look up the miter setting in the Crown Molding Table© or the Compound Miter Chart©, and subtract it from 90°.

Some saws display both miter scales. You can use either one you choose, but you *must* understand the differences between them and how to use them.

http://www.compoundmiter.com, a Quint Group company, since March 2000

Miters for Acute Corners: 0°-90°

In today's construction architecture, many homes are built with acute corners. To miter an acute corner requires that you set your saw beyond the saw's ±45° adjustment capability. Because of this, you will not be able to make a miter cut for corners less than 90° or greater than 270°, or a compound miter cut for corners less than 70° or greater than 290°. In this chapter, I will show you how to make any acute miter or acute compound miter cut.

In order to cut corners that are outside the capability of your saw, you will need to build a portable fence. A portable fence consists of nothing more than a 90° square that allows you to rotate the crown molding or trim 90° from the saw fence (see photo to the right).

In the previous chapter, I discussed the *face angle* — the angle measured from the saw fence to the blade. When using the portable fence to cut acute miters, the face angle will now be measured from the portable fence to the saw blade. If your saw has a miter scale based on the complement of the *face angle* (miter = 0° is a square cut), using the portable fence will convert your saw's miter scale to a *face angle* scale.

I'll start with the basics and explain just what you are going to do that will allow you to cut acute miters. An *acute angle* is defined as any angle that measures between 0° and 90°. If you have a 45° corner and wish to install crown molding or trim in this corner, you will need to miter the crown molding or trim at a face angle of 22.5° (45° ÷ 2 = 22.5°). Your saw will not adjust to a face angle of 22.5°. The solution to this problem is to make a portable fence.

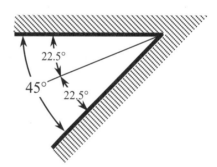

To miter, measure the corner angle and ÷ 2.

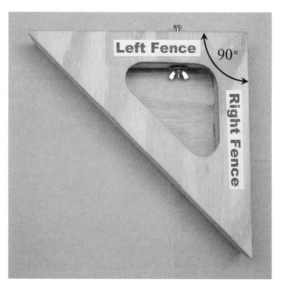

Portable Fence

To make a portable fence, you will need a 2x4 about 36" long, 1'x1' piece of 3/8" plywood, wood glue, and finishing nails. The only thing that must be exact when making your portable fence is the 90° corner. The other two corner angles and the lengths of each side are not critical.

First measure the maximum height that your saw will allow. To do that, lower your saw until it has bottomed out. Measure the vertical distance from your miter saw table to the motor, then add 1/4". From the measurement that I have made (see photo to the right), I see that my 10" compound miter saw will accommodate up to a 3-1/4" tall portable fence.

Cut all of the inner frame pieces as shown in the photo below, then assemble using wood glue and finishing nails. Again, there are only two criteria. You must have a true 90° corner (use your Exact Angle® square). Also, the finished height of your portable fence should not exceed the height capability of your saw, so remember to include the thickness of the plywood in your total height measurement.

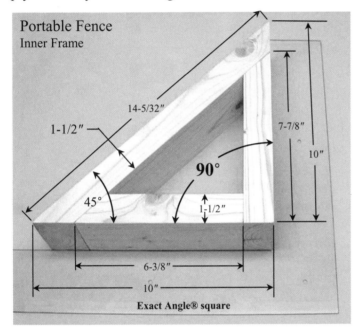

Portable Fence Inner Frame — Exact Angle® square

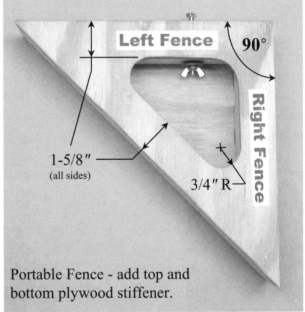

Portable Fence - add top and bottom plywood stiffener.

I have finished my portable fence. I used 3/8" plywood for my top and bottom stiffener, so I had to rip the inner frame to 2-1/2" wide (3-1/4" – 3/4" = 2-1/2"). You can use any material for the top and bottom that will accept wood glue (e.g., MDF), and it can be any thickness. However, if the thickness of the bottom of your portable fence is above the mounting hole, you will need to use wood screws instead of a bolt to attach your portable fence to your saw. Use a jig saw to cut the opening in the top of the portable fence to gain access to the wing nut, then sandpaper to smooth the rough edges.

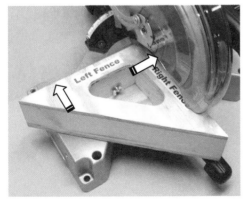

After you have finished your portable fence, check the 90° corner with your Exact Angle® square. If you find that your portable fence is not 90°, use a belt sander to remove some material so that you will have a true 90° corner.

Label your portable fence as shown, then mount it to your saw. To mount your portable fence, unplug your saw and raise your blade guard. Place the side marked "Left Fence" next to the left saw fence and slide your portable fence all the way up against the saw blade. From the back of the saw fence, push a pencil through the mounting hole to mark the portable fence, then drill a hole for your mounting bolt.

The saw I am using already has 1/4" mounting holes in it's fence. I used a 1-3/4" long 1/4" x 20 bolt, 1" flat washer, and 1/4-20 wing nut to mount my portable fence. Measure the total thickness of your saw fence and your portable fence, then add 1/2" to determine the length of the bolt you will need. To mount your portable fence to your saw's right fence, just repeat these steps for the opposite side of the saw. Again, make sure that your portable fence is held firmly against the saw fence and saw blade while marking your mounting holes.

Crown Molding - 45° Inside Corners

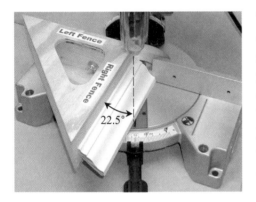

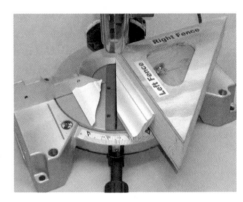

To cut the right-hand piece of a horizontal turn, 45° inside corner, you will mount your portable fence on the left saw fence (see left and right photos). Measure the corner angle with your True Angle® and divide by 2. I have my saw set at a face angle of 22.5°.

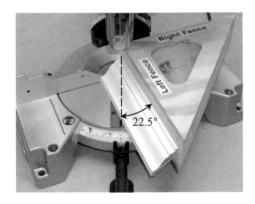

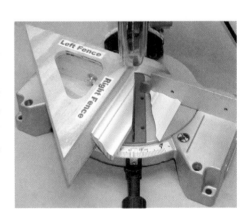

To cut the left-hand piece for your 45° inside corner, move your portable fence to the right saw fence, set the face angle on 22.5° clockwise, and make the cut.

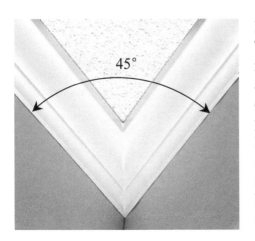

I have now installed the crown molding in my 45° inside corner. The portable fence gives you the technique needed to cut any acute miter. In this example, I used 3" crown molding. Notice in the above photos that the crown molding cut line goes all the way to the end of my blade. If you are installing 4" or larger crown molding, you will need to resort to the use of a sliding compound miter saw. If you do not have access to a larger saw, you can cut as far as your saw will allow, then finish sawing the crown molding with a hand saw. Of course, this is not the most efficient way to cut your crown, but you do not encounter acute angles very often, so it will suffice for an occasional cut.

Crown Molding - 315° Outside Corners

If you have a 45° inside corner, chances are you also have a 315° outside corner (360°- 45° = 315°). What then? You can also use your portable fence to assist you in cutting this corner. (Remember, we are dealing with the *face angle*.) To get the face angle of an outside corner, you will measure the corner angle, subtract it from 360°, then divide by 2 (360° - 315° = 45°, then ÷ by 2 = 22.5°). Note: This is the same face angle needed when cutting a 45° inside corner.

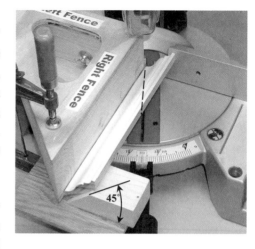

I have now set up to cut the left-hand piece of a 315° outside corner (face angle set at 22.5°). I have placed my crown molding upside down, but now it is leaning away from my portable fence. To help hold the crown while cutting, I have cut a small block as shown. The cut angle for the block will depend on the spring angle of the crown molding. I am using 45° spring angle crown and have cut this block at 45°. (If you have 38° spring angle crown, cut your block at 52°.)

To cut the opposite side (right-hand piece) of a 315° outside corner, move the portable fence to the right side of the saw, position the crown molding as shown in the photo to the left, and make the cut. I have also set my miter (face angle) clockwise to 22.5°. You now have both left-hand and right-hand pieces cut for your 315° outside corner.

By using your portable fence, you will be able to cut crown molding for corners that cannot be cut in the conventional way.

You can also cut trim (baseboard, chair rail, etc.) in a similar manner. I have attached my 3-1/4" tall portable fence to the left side of my saw, placed the trim standing upright next to it, and cut the left-hand piece for a 45° inside corner. To cut the right-hand piece, move your portable fence to the right fence of your saw.

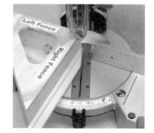

I realize that it is somewhat awkward to cut your crown molding or trim in this manner. Fortunately, even if your home has rooms that contain these odd-angled corners, you will probably not have many to cut.

Compound Miter Acute Angles

You can also cut acute angles using a compound miter cut. However, you *must* have a compound miter saw that tilts in both directions, and the *blade tilt* needed cannot exceed your saw's capability (usually ±45°, although some adjust to ±60° blade tilt).

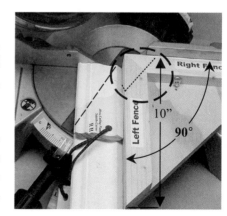

To illustrate this, I have made another portable fence (see photo to the right) using plywood, a 1x2, glue, and 1" finishing nails. Use the same criteria used earlier in this chapter. You will also locate and drill the mounting holes as we did before. **Note: *Do not* use any nails inside the dashed circle to assemble your portable fence. While using this portable fence, it will be necessary to cut through this corner.

I will first illustrate how to cut a horizontal turn, 315° outside corner, right-hand piece using 45° spring angle crown (see previous photo). From the Crown Molding Table, for a 315° outside corner, 45° crown slope angle, the blade tilt is 40.8°. Set your saw's blade tilt to the left at 40.8°. The Crown Molding Table shows a miter setting of 59.6°, but remember, the miter setting from the table is the complement of the *face angle*. You must convert this to the face angle by subtracting it from 90° (90° - 59.6° = 30.4°). Set your miter at 30.4°. Notice that I have placed my template on top of my crown molding. It allows me to confirm that I have set my saw in the correct direction to get the corner that I want to cut.

In the photo to the right, I have set up to cut a horizontal 45° inside corner, right-hand piece. My saw is tilted to the left and set on 40.8° blade tilt. The miter is set with a face angle of 30.4°.

Notice the portion of my portable fence within the dashed circle has been cut off, and the cut line for this setup extends past my saw's capability. I can finish the cut using a hand saw or by using a sliding compound miter saw.

If you encounter many of these types of cuts, the best saw to have would be a 10" or 12" sliding compound miter saw with blade tilt capability in both directions (preferably up to 60° tilt). Most radial arm saws will also make all of these cuts, so if you have access to one, you could use that.

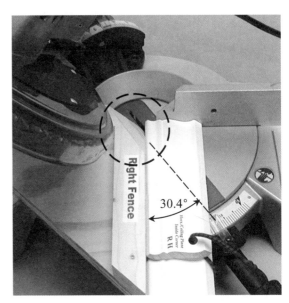

Summary and Review

If you have a corner on which to install your crown molding or trim that exceeds you saw's adjustment capability, you can easily build a portable fence that will allow you to make the cut.

The portable fence *must* have a 90° square corner and *must not* exceed the height of your saw's capability. For a 10" compound miter saw, the maximum height will be about 3-1/4" tall.

The taller 3-1/4" portable fence (photo to the right) is used for miter cuts. The shorter portable fence is for making compound miter cuts.

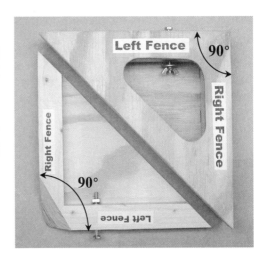

To mount your portable fence, first unplug your saw and raise the blade guard. Then position the portable fence against the saw fence and saw blade. While you are holding the portable fence in place, mark through your saw fence to the back of the portable fence, then drill your mounting hole. Repeat this for the right fence of your saw. You now have a portable fence built for your saw that will fit either side. If you wish to use this portable fence for another saw, you may need to drill new mounting holes.

You only need one mounting hole per side. This will hold your portable fence securely when you use it.

If you encounter these types of acute angle miter cuts often, you will benefit by purchasing a compound miter saw that tilts in both directions, and using the smaller portable fence that will allow you to cut your crown molding placed flat. If you need to cut crown molding 4" or larger, it would be better to use a sliding compound miter saw that tilts in both directions.

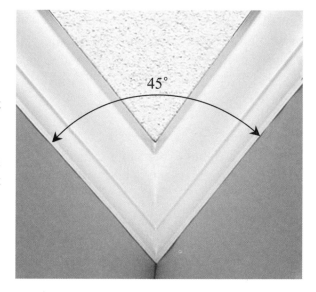

With your portable fence, you now have the ability to cut angles that exceed your saw's adjustment capability.

Remember, when you are using your portable fence, you are dealing with the *face angle* and not the complement of the face angle.

Decorative Flowerpots

Building multi-sided flowerpots has never been easier. Decorate your home with any size, small to very large. You can also have any number of sides (3 sides and up) and any wall slope angle (0° to 90°).

In this chapter, I will give you several examples of the best techniques to build small, medium, and large multi-sided flowerpots. These can be used for any number of applications ranging from huge landscape flowerpots to small decorative flowerpots for indoor use.

Large Multi-sided Flowerpots

In this example, you will be building a 41" flowerpot with 12 sides, 15" tall, and a wall slope angle of 75°. You can vary any of these specifications. The construction techniques will be the same. There are three sources to get the correct miter and blade tilt angles for the compound miter joint. You can obtain this information from the Compound Miter Chart© (Chapter 5), or the Miter Excel Program© or Flowerpots and Birdhouse Chart© (both available for purchase through our website).

I recommend using pressure-treated lumber for outdoor flowerpots. There are numerous ways to apply a finish to your flowerpot, from painting to staining. I chose to stain and apply an exterior clear finish to this flowerpot.

Sizing Your Material

Do not let these tables scare you. To get the dimensions for building your flowerpot to your specifications, you just multiply two numbers together. I will walk you through the example for a large 41" flowerpot step-by-step and show you how easy it is to make.

Figure 1 shows the various dimensions associated with building a flowerpot. Size, number of sides, height, and wall slope angle are all your choice. Then, using your specifications, Tables 3, 4, and 5 (this chapter), and the Compound Miter Chart (Chapter 5), you can derive the width, length, miter angle, and the blade tilt you need.

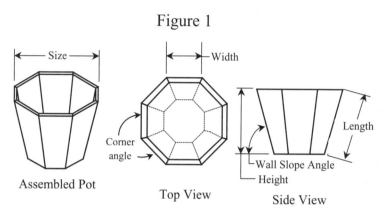

Figure 1

Assembled Pot   Top View   Side View

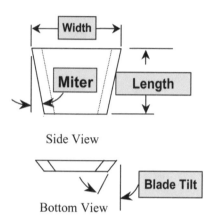

Side View

Bottom View

The drawing to the left shows a typical wall piece. Before you can cut any of these, you need to determine the dimensions and angles needed.

Let's start by calculating the width of each wall piece for the 41" flowerpot. From Table 3 (for 12 sides), you see that the width-to-size ratio for our example is 0.268. Now multiply the size you want by this ratio to get the width (41" X 0.268 = 11"). Therefore, W (width) = 11".

Table 3 — Width Vs. Size

Size

12 W=Size x .268

# of Sides	Width to Size	# of Sides	Width to Size
3	1.155	17	0.185
4	1.000	18	0.176
5	0.650	19	0.166
6	0.577	20	0.158
7	0.456	21	0.150
8	0.414	22	0.144
9	0.353	23	0.137
10	0.325	24	0.132
11	0.288	25	0.126
12	0.268	26	0.121
13	0.243	27	0.116
14	0.228	28	0.113
15	0.210	29	0.108
16	0.199	30	0.105

Let's do a few more examples to make sure you understand how to use Table 3. What would be the width of each wall piece if you wanted an 18" flowerpot with 8 sides? From Table 3 (for 8 sides), you see that the width-to-size ratio is 0.414. Multiply the size you want (18") times this ratio. (Answer: 18" x 0.414 = 7.45") Now try a 96" flowerpot with 30 sides. (Answer: 10.08") For the last example, let's do a 4.5" flowerpot with 10 sides. (Answer: 1.46")

Table 4 - Length to Height Ratio

Wall Slope Angle	L/H Ratio	Wall Slope Angle	L/H Ratio	Wall Slope Angle	L/H Ratio	Wall Slope Angle	L/H Ratio	Wall Slope Angle	L/H Ratio	Wall Slope Angle	L/H Ratio
1	57.299	16	3.628	31	1.942	46	1.390	61	1.143	76	1.031
2	28.654	17	3.420	32	1.887	47	1.367	62	1.133	77	1.026
3	19.107	18	3.236	33	1.836	48	1.346	63	1.122	78	1.022
4	14.336	19	3.072	34	1.788	49	1.325	64	1.113	79	1.019
5	11.474	20	2.924	35	1.743	50	1.305	65	1.103	80	1.015
6	9.567	21	2.790	36	1.701	51	1.287	66	1.095	81	1.012
7	8.206	22	2.669	37	1.662	52	1.269	67	1.086	82	1.010
8	7.185	23	2.559	38	1.624	53	1.252	68	1.079	83	1.008
9	6.392	24	2.459	39	1.589	54	1.236	69	1.071	84	1.006
10	5.759	25	2.366	40	1.556	55	1.221	70	1.064	85	1.004
11	5.241	26	2.281	41	1.524	56	1.206	71	1.058	86	1.002
12	4.810	27	2.203	42	1.494	57	1.192	72	1.051	87	1.001
13	4.445	28	2.130	43	1.466	58	1.179	73	1.046	88	1.001
14	4.134	29	2.063	44	1.440	59	1.167	74	1.040	89	1.000
15	3.864	30	2.000	45	1.414	60	1.155	75	1.035	90	1.000

Now let's derive the length needed for the 41" flowerpot. I chose a wall slope angle of 75°. From Table 4, the length-to-height ratio for a 75° wall slope angle is 1.035. To get the length, multiply the height you want by this ratio (L = 15" x 1.035 = 15.5").

In order to cut the joints, the last bits of information needed are the miter and blade tilt angles. To get these angles, use Table 5 (to the right) and the Compound Miter Chart© (Chapter 5). To use the Compound Miter Chart©, you need to know the angle formed by the outside corners of the flowerpot and the wall slope angle. You already know that the wall slope angle for the 41" flowerpot is 75°. Table 5 will provide the outside corner angle. From Table 5 (for 12 sides), you see that the outside corner angle is 210°. From the Compound Miter Chart©, using 210° as the corner angle and 75° as the wall slope angle (the wall slope angle is labeled crown slope angle in the Compound Miter Chart©), we get miter angle = 4° and blade tilt = 14.5°. You now have all the dimensions and angles to start cutting the flowerpot.

Note: The Miter Excel Program© has all of this programmed. When you enter your specifications, the program makes the calculations for you. You simply print the results and work from the printout in your workshop.

Table 5 - # of Sides Vs. Corner Angle			
# of Sides	Corner Angle	# of Sides	Corner Angle
3	300.0	17	201.2
4	270.0	18	200.0
5	252.0	19	198.9
6	240.0	20	198.0
7	231.4	21	197.1
8	225.0	22	196.4
9	220.0	23	195.7
10	216.0	24	195.0
11	212.7	25	194.4
12	210.0	26	193.8
13	207.7	27	193.3
14	205.7	28	192.9
15	204.0	29	192.4
16	202.5	30	192.0

From the information you have derived, you know the width = 11", length = 15.5", miter = 4°, and blade tilt = 14.5°. Since each wall piece is 15.5" long and you need 12 pieces, a 2x12 16' long will be needed to cut all 12 sides of the flowerpot. Be sure to handpick through the stack of lumber to find a straight board. I highly recommend that you purchase treated lumber that has not been stored outside. This will cut down on the amount of warpage the lumber will have when it is dry.

Cutting the Material

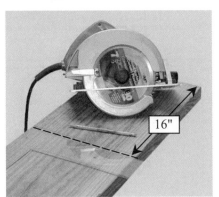

You are now ready to cut out each piece of the 41" flowerpot. Start by cutting the 2x12 into twelve 16" pieces.

As an optional step, you can run these through a thickness planer until both sides are smooth.

The boards that you will be cutting are too large for a compound miter saw. You will need to use a table saw.

Now square the edges of the boards. Check the square of your saw blade before you begin. Make sure it is 90° with the table. First rip the boards to a width of 11-1/4". Set your fence and run all 12 boards through, cutting only one side. Then move the fence so the cut will be 11-1/8" wide. Turn the boards around and cut the opposite side of all 12 boards. You now have both sides of your boards parallel and square.

Mark each side as to which you prefer to be the outside top and bottom. You will use these markings for the remaining cuts to position your wall pieces as shown in the pictures.

Next square the ends of each board. Take off about half the thickness of the saw blade with each pass. Clamp a 1x6 to the table, which will allow you to cut off about 1/16" on each pass. Cut as many passes as needed to square the end of the board. This end also will be the bottom of the flowerpot that will sit on the ground when finished. Cut all 12 pieces in this manner.

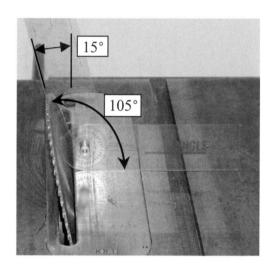

So far you have both sides and the bottom of each piece squared. The next step will be to cut the top. You will want the top of the flowerpot to be level when assembled. The wall slope angle for this pot is 75°. Therefore, you will need to tilt the saw blade 15° from vertical (90°-75° = 15°) in order to make the top level when assembled. Use your True Angle® tool to check the 15° blade tilt (90°+15°=105°).

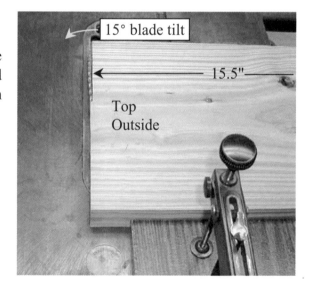

Cut the top of each wall piece at 15.5". You must have the top outside of the wall facing up and the saw blade tilted 15° from vertical to the left. Continue cutting 12 pieces in exactly the same manner.

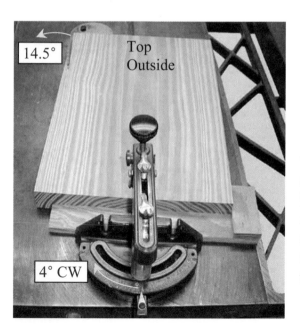

You are now ready to cut the compound miter angle on each side of the wall piece. You can build a very simple jig to help in cutting all the wall pieces the same. It consists of a 2" strip of plywood with a 90° stop which is glued and stapled to the end. With the miter and blade tilt angles set, slide the jig from side to side so the saw blade just cuts into the upper left edge of the wall piece as shown. Then clamp the jig to your miter. Cut all 12 pieces the same, making sure you have each wall piece positioned in the jig as shown. The miter angle = 4° and the blade tilt = 14.5° for the flowerpot you are building. Check the angle of your blade and miter setting with your True Angle® tool. This is the most critical measurement you have for building the flowerpot. Any error in setting these two angles will be evident in all 12 joints when finished.

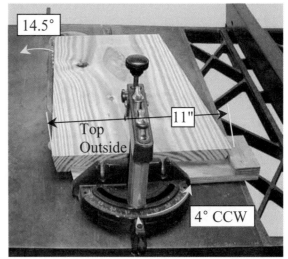

To cut the opposite side of the wall piece, rotate the miter 4° in the counter-clockwise direction from 0°. The blade tilt has not changed. This time position your jig so the cut will give you an 11" width at the top. (Be sure you position the wall piece in the jig as shown.) Make the first cut wide enough so as not to have the top width less than 11". Then adjust your jig and make another cut on the same side. When you have 11" as the width, tighten the jig down and cut the remaining wall pieces.

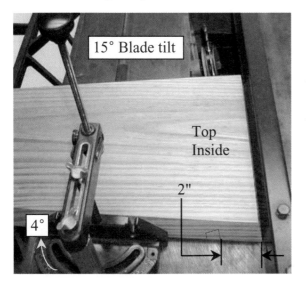

You should now have all of the wall pieces cut to size. Both sides should already be cut with a miter of 4° and a blade tilt of 14.5°. The bottom edge should be cut square and the top should have a 15° bevel cut. You should now make the top and bottom outside dado cut. Assume you will be using 3/4" grass rope in the final assembly, and cut the dado 3/4" wide and 3/8" deep (half the diameter of the rope). Choose to start the dado 2" below the top of the flowerpot. Tilt the dado blade 15° in the direction the top of the wall is beveled. Make several test cuts on a scrap piece of wood to get all of the adjustments set before using any of the flowerpot pieces. If you do not have a dado blade to make the 3/4" cut, you can make the same cut with your saw by moving the fence the thickness of your saw blade and making several cuts. It is easier to cut all 12 pieces the same before moving the fence.

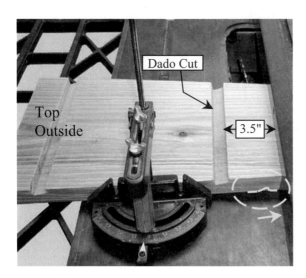

If you are going to install a bottom in your flowerpot, the next step will be to cut a dado on the bottom inside of each piece. This photo shows the two outside dado cuts, and the board positioned to cut a dado for the bottom. The blade tilt of 15° will be the same. Since this is the bottom, make the dado cut flush on one side with the inside surface.

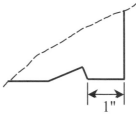

The bottom will fit in the notch made by the dado cut. You will not be installing a bottom for this example, but I wanted to make the dado cuts to show you how it's done.

Flowerpot Assembly

You are now ready to assemble your flowerpot. The easiest way to do this is to prop all of the pieces against a round object so you can insert a ratchet strap in the dado cuts. In my workshop, I just happen to have a 36" diameter piece of plywood left over from another project. I placed the plywood on three paint cans and propped all 12 pieces of the flowerpot up against it. I then placed my ratchet strap in the dado groove as shown. Place a pad under each ratchet to protect the wood because the straps need to be tight.

Both ratchet straps are now installed and tightened. You now need to adjust the joints so they line up properly. Use a rubber mallet to tap the pieces into place. (If you need to use a hammer, you should pad it to prevent denting the wood.) Adjust from the inside only. Because the ratchet straps are very tight, it is much easier to tap from the inside for your adjustments. If an edge or corner is too far inward, tap it out from the inside. If you go too far, tap the adjacent piece out to match it. Once you have all of your joints adjusted, tighten the ratchet straps again.

You are now ready to glue all of the joints. Waterproof glue is expensive but preferred. Turn your flowerpot up on its side. If you do not have the ratchet straps tight enough, the flowerpot will collapse.

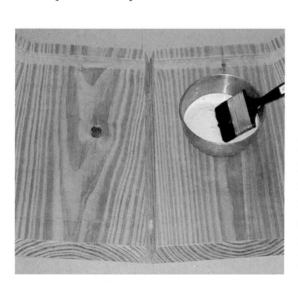

Press gently on the two adjacent pieces to open the joint, insert the glue and roll the flowerpot to the side to open the next joint. Glue the joints quickly, because some final adjustments will be required when you finish gluing. Glue all 12 joints, and turn the flowerpot on its top, and make any adjustments to the joints using your rubber mallet or padded hammer. Remove any excess glue and let it dry overnight.

For outdoor use, I would not recommend using glue alone to hold a flowerpot together. There are several ways you can add additional strength to the joints. I have chosen to use a heavy-duty steel-banding strap. You could also use nails or screws. Finishing nails can be driven into the joints from both directions. Screws should be inserted into the dado grooves from both directions. You should also pre-drill all holes.

Finishing Nails (Alternative)

The flowerpot is assembled and ready for the finish to be applied. I have stained the wood and applied several coats of exterior varnish.

To help protect the wood from moisture, coat the inside of the flowerpot with foundation sealer (optional), then staple 6mil plastic (plastic not shown) over the foundation sealer. You can also use roofing tarpaper instead of 6mil plastic.

Total cost for the flowerpot: $50. Plants and potting soil: $50.

Medium/Small Flowerpots

There are several different ways in which you can build flowerpots in the medium-to-small size range. The flowerpot can be painted or stained. You can make the flowerpot from rectangular board stock material (flat on both sides), or use material such as crown molding where you have a preference as to which side of your material is the outside of the flowerpot. Another choice you need to make is whether or not you want the top and/or bottom horizontal (beveled), as was the large flowerpot we made at the beginning of this chapter.

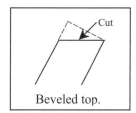

Beveled top.

I will walk you through building this flowerpot step by step and provide examples of the best way to set up and cut your material.

Here we have an 8-sided, 10" size flowerpot, 4" tall with a 65° wall slope angle.

The wood grain pattern on my stock material had a favorable pattern on one side. I wanted that side to be the outside of the flowerpot. If you were using crown molding as your stock material, you would use this same technique.

Sizing Your Material

Regardless of how you want to build your flowerpot, you will start with the same size stock material. First, determine the dimensions just as you did with the large flowerpot.

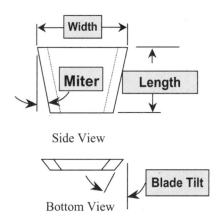

Side View

Bottom View

The **width** of each wall piece can be obtained by using Table 3. The size of this flowerpot is 10". Therefore, the Width = 10" x 0.414 = 4.14".

The **length** of each wall piece depends on the height (4") of the flowerpot and the wall slope angle (65°). From Table 4 the Length = 4" (height) x 1.103 (65° wall slope) = 4.4".

From Table 5 we get 225° as the outside corner angle for 8 sides. To get the miter and blade tilt angles, use the Compound Miter Chart© (Chapter 5) using 225° as the corner angle and 65° as the crown/wall slope angle. The miter angle is 10° and the blade tilt angle is 20.3°.

You now have all of the dimensions of each wall piece. Start with a 1x6 board about 45" long (4.14" wide x 8 pieces = approximately 33", then add 12".) The Miter Excel Program© will calculate all of these dimensions for you and is available for purchase/download through our website.

Cutting the Material

There are two methods for cutting your stock material. Method #1 should be used if you want to paint your flowerpot and are using rectangular stock material (flat on both sides). You can also choose to bevel the top or not. This method requires that you flip the stock over between each cut.

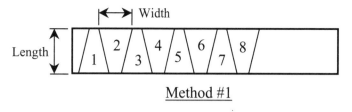

Method #1

Method #2 should be used if you want one side of your stock material, usually the best side, facing outward on the flowerpot. If you want to apply a natural wood finish and one side of the board has a desirable wood grain,

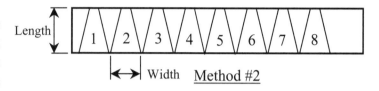

Method #2

you would use this method. You can also choose either to bevel the top and/or bottom or leave it square. This method would also apply if you are using crown molding or any type of stock material that is not the same on both sides.

Method 1 – Material Flat Both Sides

Let's go through Method 1 step by step. Remember to turn your stock material over each time you make a cut.

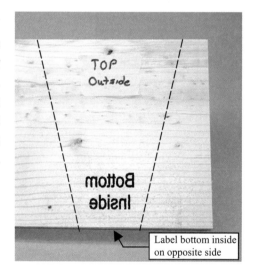

Step 1. Label your stock material Top/Outside and Bottom/Inside as shown. This will make it easier to explain how to position your material on your saw. Label the right end of your board stock. This is very important if you are going to bevel the top and bottom edges of your pot so they will be horizontal when finished. If you are not going to bevel the top and bottom of your flowerpot, you can skip to Step 4. I will bevel the top and bottom of this example.

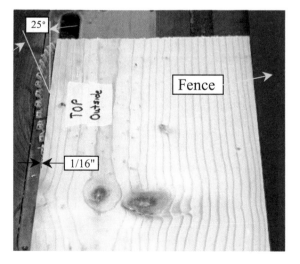

Step 2. To bevel the edge of your stock, tilt your saw blade. Since the flowerpot wall slopes 65°, you will need to tilt the saw blade 25° from vertical (90° - 65° = 25°). Adjust your fence so you are cutting very little of the top surface (approximately 1/16").

Step 3. The next cut will be made on the opposite edge by turning the stock material over and placing as shown. The bottom inside, which you labeled in Step 2, should now be next to the blade. Adjust your fence so that you will be making the final length cut of each wall piece as determined earlier (4.4"). Make this bevel cut with the same blade tilt (25°).

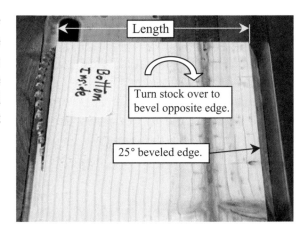

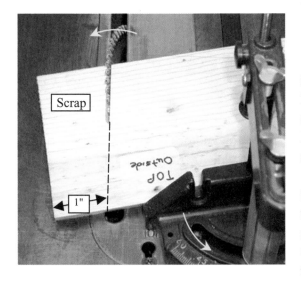

Step 4. If you chose to bevel the edges of your stock in Steps 2 and 3, you are ready to continue with Step 4. Your stock should be already cut to the correct dimension of 4.4" wide. If you did not intend to bevel the edges, you need to rip your stock to 4.4" wide (saw blade vertical).

Set your miter to 10° counter-clockwise and adjust the blade tilt to the left to 20.3° as shown. Position your stock material as shown and make the first cut. Be sure you have the Top/Outside label next to the miter gauge. Save the scrap piece to use as a jig in the next step.

Step 5. Turn your material over and position as shown. The Bottom/Inside label should be next to your miter gauge. Adjust the material to the right or left to get the correct width of each wall piece (4.14" top outside). Clamp the scrap piece as shown. The scrap piece will now serve as a jig to cut the remaining pieces. To make the next cut, turn the stock material over and realign it to the jig. Continue until all 8 pieces are cut.

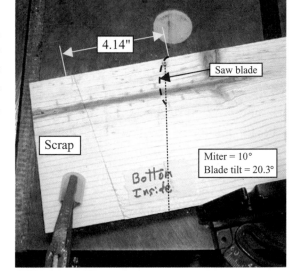

Assembly

Step 6. You are now ready to assemble your flowerpot for gluing. The best way to do this is to place several tight rubber bands around the outside of the flowerpot. If you have made your flowerpot with a wall slope angle less than 75°, you will have difficulty keeping the rubber bands from slipping off the tapered end. You could cut a groove on the outside of each piece about 1" from the top and bottom to hold the rubber bands, or you can use stiff wire clips as shown above. These are made from a coat hanger and are just long enough to reach halfway down the flowerpot. Tape one to each wall piece.

Place each wall piece around a round object to allow you to get the first few rubber bands in place. Here I have used a quart paint can. You can now remove the paint can and add a few more rubber bands. The wire clips will keep the rubber bands from slipping off. You can also use several wraps of string.

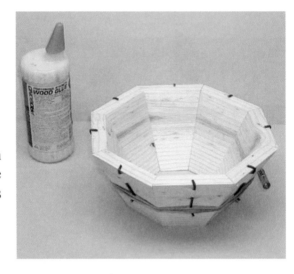

Place the flowerpot on its side and press down just enough to open one of the joints on the inside. Then insert some glue. Do this to each joint. Make any final alignments between each wall piece and let dry overnight.

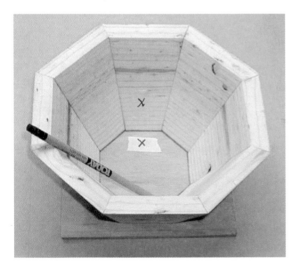

Step 7. To add a bottom to your flowerpot, trace the bottom opening onto a piece of material. For the best fit, mark the matching edges so you can install the bottom exactly as drawn.

Draw a second line outside the first about the distance of the thickness of the bottom material (1/4" in this example).

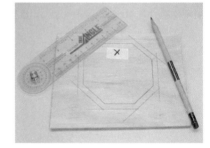

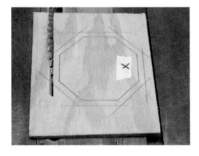

Tilt the saw blade to 25° (90° - 65° = 25°). Keep the bottom on the right side of the blade and cut along the outside line for all 8 sides.

Check-fit the bottom and trim if necessary to get the fit you want. When you have the bottom cut to your satisfaction, glue it in place. Your flowerpot is now ready to paint/finish.

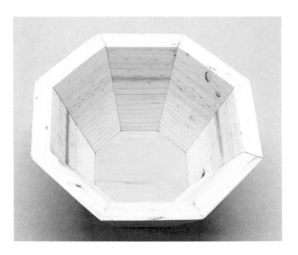

Method 2 – Best Side Out

There are a lot of similarities between Methods 1 and 2. I will reference the above steps when they are identical.

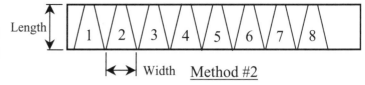

Method #2

For this example, you will make the same size flowerpot that you did for the example in Method 1. The stock material you start with will be a 1x6 about 45" long (same as Method 1). Review and repeat Steps 1 through 4 above. (Both methods are the same until Step 5.)

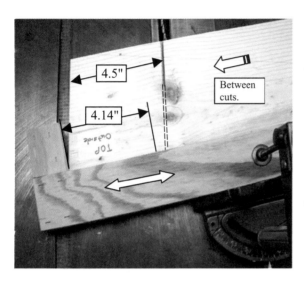

Step 5. Place your stock material in your cutting jig as shown. The top width needed is 4.14". Adjust your cutting jig and cut each piece about 4.5" wide. Do not turn your stock over between each cut as we did in Method 1.

The jig I use to cut flowerpots is shown in the picture below. This is made from three layers of ½" plywood glued together for a total thickness of 1.5". It is best not to assemble the jig with nails, because you would probably cut into one while you are using it.

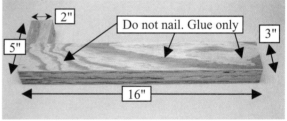

Cut all 8 pieces by removing the piece you just cut and sliding the stock material into position for the next cut.

To cut the other side of each wall piece, rotate the miter to 10° clockwise. The blade tilt will remain set at 20.3°. Place the wall piece you have marked as Top/Outside in the jig and align it so the saw blade will just cut into the upper right corner. Stack all of the remaining pieces so they are oriented in the same manner as the one marked Top/Outside. When you have cut the first piece, remove it and position the next one exactly the same. Cut all pieces the same way. You should now have all of the 8 wall pieces cut and ready to assemble. If you were using crown molding to make this pot, you would have all pieces cut with the flat side of the crown on the inside of the box.

Follow Steps 6 and 7 in Method #1 to assemble the flowerpot. You are now ready to apply your choice of finish.

Small Decorative Flowerpots

You can make these small decorative pots from any of your crown molding scraps. The specifications for this pot are as follows: size = 6", wall slope angle = 80° and height = 4-5/8". The lid for this pot is at a wall slope angle = 10°. I used 5" crown molding. The decals and decorative knob can be purchased from any craft store.

When using crown molding to build flowerpots, follow the procedure used for making medium to small flowerpots, Method 2. You will not be able to turn the long piece of crown over and cut the adjacent piece. Cut each piece separately.

Summary and Review

There are multiple ways to cut flowerpot wall pieces. I have provided what I feel are the best and easiest directions to follow. When building very large flowerpots, the material used is often too large to handle and needs to be cut into individual pieces before you begin. For smaller flowerpots, you can use Method 1 or Method 2 to cut your wall pieces depending on the type of material you are using and the type of finish you plan to apply.

Regardless of the method used to cut the material, you will need to determine the flowerpot wall-piece dimensions. Let's review how to calculate each one.

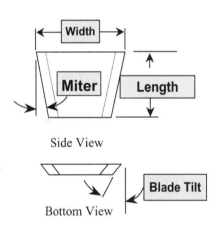

Side View

Bottom View

Width: The width of each wall section depends on the size and number of sides you choose (See Table 3). For example, for a 25" flowerpot with 10 sides, Width = 25" x 0.325 = 8.125"

Length: The length of each wall section is dependent on the height of the flowerpot and the wall slope angle you choose (See Table 4). For example, an 18" high flowerpot with a wall slope angle of 50°, Length = 18" x 1.305 = 23.5"

Miter and Blade Tilt Angles: The miter and blade tilt angles depend on the number of sides and the wall slope angle you choose. Use Table 5 and the Compound Miter Chart©. To use the Compound Miter Chart©, you need the corner angle of the flowerpot. Table 5 provides corner angles versus number of sides. For example, 12 sides have an outside corner angle of 210°. From the Compound Miter Chart©, use a corner angle of 210° and a wall slope angle of 75° to get the miter = 4°, blade tilt = 14.5°.

The Miter Excel Program©, available for purchase through our website, has all of these calculations. You simply type in size, number of sides, height, and wall slope angle desired, and press enter. All of the dimensions are calculated and displayed. Then print the page and take the drawing to your workshop.

Here are a couple of other examples of what you can build using the compound miter information in this chapter. The windmill base is nothing more than an inverted 15" flowerpot with 8 sides, and is 24" high with a wall slope angle of 85°. The lighthouse is a 12" flowerpot with 6 sides and is 18" high with a wall slope angle of 80°. If you enjoy building items like these, you now have all of the information to cut any compound miter angle you need.

Birdhouses and Gazebos

If you enjoy having birds in your yard, you will love building gazebo-style birdhouses or birdfeeders. These make great gifts for family and friends. You can now build any style you like using the information contained in this chapter.

This gazebo birdfeeder is 20" x 20" x 24" high. The top lifts off to allow the addition of 6 lbs. of birdseed. The roof has 4 sides with a 40° wall slope angle (miter angle = 37.5°, blade tilt = 27°). The entire birdfeeder contains 123 individual pieces of wood.

To the right is an 8-sided birdhouse with a 45° wall slope angle for the roof. The walls of the birdhouse are cut to 22.5° and the top of the walls are beveled to 45° to match the roof slope. The birdhouse has a removable bottom for easy cleaning.

This is a 6-sided birdhouse. The roof has a 15° slope angle and the walls have a 75° slope angle. Compare the bottom of this birdhouse to a flowerpot. They are the same. The tops of the walls were cut with a 30° blade tilt so they match the roof slope. The decorations are rub-on decals available from most craft stores.

This is an 8-sided birdhouse. It has a 15° roof slope angle and a 75° wall slope angle.

Would you like to build a fancy gazebo but are not sure how to cut all of the necessary angles correctly? Our compound miter products will provide all the angles. This gazebo has 8 sides with a 15° roof slope.

Cutting the Material for a Birdhouse/Gazebo

Let's set up and cut the material to build a 4-sided, 8" birdhouse roof with a 45° wall slope angle. Flowerpots and birdhouses are almost identical in the way you determine the dimensions and angles needed to cut the material. A birdhouse roof is nothing more than a flowerpot that is tall enough for the walls come to a point. I will be referring to the steps in Chapter 15 while explaining how to cut a birdhouse roof.

Table 6 - Gazebo Pyramid Wall Slope Angle Vs. Length / Size Ratio											
Wall Slope Angle	L/S Ratio	Wall Slope Angle	L/S Ratio	Wall Slope Angle	L/S Ratio	Wall Slope Angle	L/S Ratio	Wall Slope Angle	L/S Ratio	Wall Slope Angle	L/S Ratio
1	0.500	16	0.520	31	0.583	46	0.720	61	1.031	76	2.067
2	0.500	17	0.523	32	0.590	47	0.733	62	1.065	77	2.223
3	0.501	18	0.526	33	0.596	48	0.747	63	1.101	78	2.405
4	0.501	19	0.529	34	0.603	49	0.762	64	1.141	79	2.620
5	0.502	20	0.532	35	0.610	50	0.778	65	1.183	80	2.879
6	0.503	21	0.536	36	0.618	51	0.795	66	1.229	81	3.196
7	0.504	22	0.539	37	0.626	52	0.812	67	1.280	82	3.593
8	0.505	23	0.543	38	0.635	53	0.831	68	1.335	83	4.103
9	0.506	24	0.547	39	0.643	54	0.851	69	1.395	84	4.783
10	0.508	25	0.552	40	0.653	55	0.872	70	1.462	85	5.737
11	0.509	26	0.556	41	0.663	56	0.894	71	1.536	86	7.168
12	0.511	27	0.561	42	0.673	57	0.918	72	1.618	87	9.554
13	0.513	28	0.566	43	0.684	58	0.944	73	1.710	88	14.33
14	0.515	29	0.572	44	0.695	59	0.971	74	1.814	89	28.65
15	0.518	30	0.577	45	0.707	60	1.000	75	1.932	90	N/A

Table 6 provides the relation between the size desired and the length needed to form a pyramid. In order to cut our stock material, we need to know the length to make each roof piece. To use Table 6, locate the desired wall slope angle. Then multiply the corresponding length/size ratio and the size desired. Let's work an example.

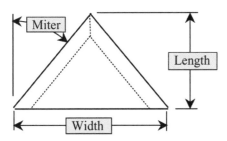

Typical dimensions for a pyramid roof.

This is a typical shape of a roof piece for a gazebo. In this example, you are building an 8" roof with a 45° wall slope angle. Referencing Table 6, you see that for a wall slope angle of 45° the length/size ratio is 0.707. Therefore, the length needed for the pyramid in this example is 8" x 0.707= 5.66". You will need to cut the stock material 5-5/8" wide. (I have provided a fraction-to-decimal conversion table in Chapter 17.)

Let's do a few more examples. What length would be needed for an 18" pyramid roof with a 60° wall slope angle? L = 18" x 1.000 = 18". What about a 5" roof with a wall slope angle of 25°? L = 5" x 0.552 = 2.76". Now try a 12" roof with a wall slope angle of 10°. L = 12" x 0.508 = 6.1". To get the remaining angles and dimensions, you will be using Tables 3 and 5 in Chapter 15 and the Compound Miter Chart© in Chapter 5. Now derive all the dimensions and angles needed to build your birdhouse roof.

Width: The width of each roof piece depends on the size you want and the number of sides you choose. (see Table 3). For example, for an 8" roof with 4 sides, Width = 8" x 1.000 = 8".

Length: The length of each roof piece depends on the size you want and the roof slope angle you choose. From Table 6, for 8" size and 45° roof slope, Length = 8" x 0.707 = 5.66".

Miter and Blade Tilt Angles: The miter and blade tilt angles depend on the number of sides and the wall slope angle you choose. Use Table 5 and the Compound Miter Chart© (Chapter 5). To use the Compound Miter Chart©, you need the corner angle of the pyramid roof. Table 5 provides corner angles versus number of sides. For example, a 4-sided roof has a corner angle of 270°. From the Compound Miter Chart©, use a corner angle of 270° and a wall slope angle of 45° to get the miter = 35.3° and blade tilt = 30.0°. You are now ready to cut the material.

The Miter Excel Program© has all of these calculations programmed. You just type in size, number of sides, the wall slope angle desired, and press enter. All of the dimensions are then calculated and displayed.

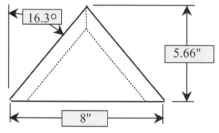

Dimensions needed for our example.

You need 4 of these roof pieces. If you intend to paint this birdhouse and the stock material is the same on both sides, make the cuts using Method 1 in Chapter 15.

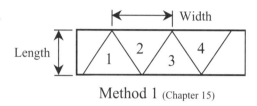

Method 1 (Chapter 15)

Cut your stock material 5.66" wide and about 30" long. Remove the first cut, then align and clamp it to your table saw to use as a guide for cutting the remaining pieces. When you are cutting a pyramid roof where the top comes to a point, it will be necessary to trim off about 1/4" of the stock material between each cut to true the saw cut surface. Continue until all pieces are cut.

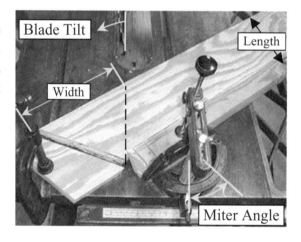

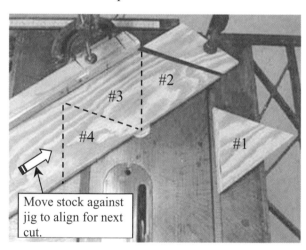

Move stock against jig to align for next cut.

The vertical walls of the 4-sided birdhouse are 6" wide with a wall slope angle of 90°. To get the bevel for the corners (270° outside corner) look up the corner angle in the Miter Table© (Chapter 3). The bevel (blade tilt) is 45°. For the 8-sided birdhouse, the width is 2.5" (Table 3, 6"x.414 = 2.5").

From Table 5, we see that the outside corner angle for 8 sides is 225° and from the Miter Table, we get a bevel (blade tilt) of 22.5°. To assemble, see Chapter 15. You will also want to install removable bottoms in the birdhouses. You are now ready to paint and enjoy your new creations.

http://www.compoundmiter.com, a Quint Group company, since March 2000

Summary and Review

When building very large birdhouses or birdfeeders, the material used is often too large to handle and needs to be cut into individual pieces before you begin. For smaller birdhouses/birdfeeders, you can use Method 1 or 2 (Chapter 15) to cut your roof pieces, depending on the type of material you are using and the type of finish you apply.

Regardless of how you cut the material, you will need to determine the dimensions. Let's review how to calculate each one.

Width: The width of each roof piece depends on the size and the number of sides you choose (Table 3). For example, an 8" roof with 4 sides, Width = 8" x 1.000 = 8". For an 8" roof with 8 sides, Width = 8" x 0.414 = 3.3"

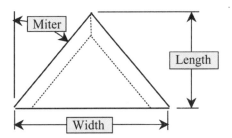

Typical dimensions for a pyramid roof.

Length: The length of each roof piece depends on the size and the roof slope angle you choose (Table 6). For a roof slope angle of 45°, you get a length-to-size ratio of 0.707. Therefore, for an 8" roof with a slope angle of 45°, Length = 8" x 0.707 = 5.656" or approximately 5-5/8". (The length calculation is the only difference between flowerpots and birdhouses. For a birdhouse you want a pyramid.)

Miter and Blade Tilt Angles: The miter and blade tilt angles depend on the number of sides and the roof slope angle. Use Table 5 and the Compound Miter Chart©. To use the Compound Miter Chart©, you need the corner angle of the birdhouse roof. Table 5 provides corner angles versus number of sides. For example, a four-sided roof has a corner angle of 270°. From the Compound Miter Chart©, use a corner angle of 270° and a wall slope angle of 45° to get miter = 35.3° and blade tilt = 30.0°.

Children and adults alike love these birdhouses/birdfeeders, and with the information contained in Chapters 15 and 16, you will be able to make any style you like. Be sure to review the birdhouse links on my website. There you can get all sorts of information on birdhouses and how to feed the birds you would like to attract.

Definitions, Tables, and Charts

In this chapter, I have assembled all of the definitions, tables and charts needed to install crown molding and trim. I have also included conversion tables that will allow you to easily convert fractions of an inch to decimals of an inch, and roof pitch to roof slope in degrees.

Definitions

There are a few simple definitions you need to understand in order to install crown molding. All of the defined angles are displayed in the picture below. I have used these definitions throughout this book and on all of our compound miter products.

Spring Angle

The **crown spring angle** is the angle measured from the back of the crown to the wall. Crown is manufactured to be installed with the bottom of the crown held firmly against the wall. The two common spring angles are 38° and 45°. There are other crown moldings with different spring angles. ***Check the spring angle of your crown.*** (See page 34.)

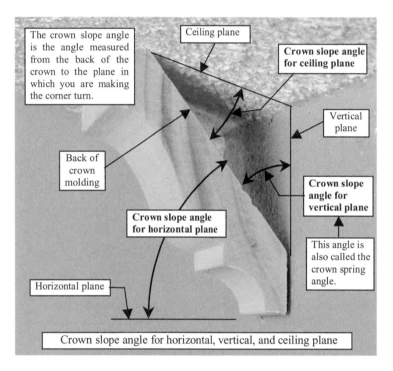

The crown slope angle is the angle measured from the back of the crown to the plane in which you are making the corner turn.

Ceiling plane

Crown slope angle for ceiling plane

Vertical plane

Back of crown molding

Crown slope angle for vertical plane

Crown slope angle for horizontal plane

This angle is also called the crown spring angle.

Horizontal plane

Crown slope angle for horizontal, vertical, and ceiling plane

Horizontal Plane

A **horizontal plane** is a flat surface that is parallel to the floor. If you are installing crown on a horizontal ceiling, all of the turns made with your crown molding are in a horizontal plane.

Vertical Plane

A **vertical plane** is simply the wall on which you are mounting the crown molding or trim. You turn the crown in the vertical plane any time you turn the crown or trim up or down (e.g., cathedral/vaulted ceilings, stairs, etc.). See page 42 for an explanation of how to get the corner angles for a vertical plane turn.

Ceiling Plane

The **ceiling plane** is the flat surface that is the ceiling itself. At times, you will turn your crown molding in the ceiling plane when working with a cathedral/vaulted ceiling. There are pros and cons associated with making turns in the ceiling plane (Chapter 5).

Crown Slope Angles

Crown Slope Angle for a Horizontal Plane

The **crown slope angle for a horizontal plane** is the angle measured from the back of the crown to a horizontal plane (the floor) when turning the crown horizontally. If you are using crown molding with a 38° spring angle, the crown slope angle for a horizontal turn (horizontal ceiling) is 52° (90°-38° = 52°). If you are using crown molding with a 45° spring angle, the crown slope angle for a horizontal turn is 45°.

Crown Slope Angle for a Vertical Plane

The **crown slope angle for a vertical plane** is the angle measured from the back of the crown to the wall when turning the crown up or down. Any time you are working with a cathedral/vaulted ceiling (or even staircase trim), you will need to turn upward or downward. If you are using 38° spring angle crown, the crown slope angle is 38° for vertical turns (vertical plane). If you are using 45° spring angle crown, the crown slope angle is 45° for vertical turns.

Crown Slope Angle for a Ceiling Plane

The **crown slope angle for a ceiling plane** is the angle measured from the back of the crown to the ceiling when turning the crown in the plane of the ceiling. This is the most confusing of all the crown slope angles because it depends on the slope of your ceiling and whether you are running the crown along the horizontal wall or along the sloped wall. I have provided three examples below using 52°/38° crown (38° spring angle). If you have 45°/45° crown (45° spring angle), the crown slope angles for these examples would be 45°-20° = 25°, 45°, and 45°+20° = 65°.

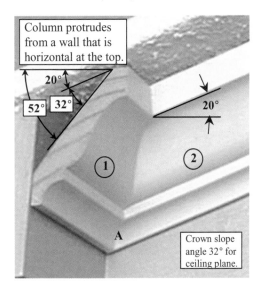

Cathedral Ceiling - Horizontal Wall
Crown slope angle is 32° when turning in the plane of a 20° upward-sloped ceiling.

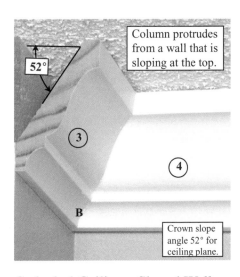

Cathedral Ceiling - Sloped Wall
Crown slope angle is 52° when turning in the plane of the ceiling.

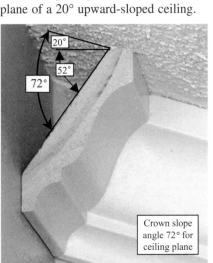

Cathedral Ceiling - Horizontal Wall
Crown slope angle is 72° when turning in the plane of a 20° downward-sloped ceiling.

You should only turn your crown in the plane of the ceiling when you are making short runs and will soon be turning the crown back in the original direction. When making outside corner turns in the ceiling plane on a cathedral/vaulted ceiling such as when wrapping a column, you will be able to eliminate the small wedge piece needed for horizontal to vertical turns. When you turn the crown in the ceiling plane, you change it's spring angle. If you turn the crown back to the original direction, the spring angle will return to the correct angle.

Miter Table©

The Miter Table© is for use with a miter saw (blade will not tilt). This table applies to any trim that lies flat on the surface when installed. This includes baseboards, chair rails, quarter and half round trim, cove molding, corner molding, fireplace trim, and door and window casings. Measure the corner angle where the trim will be installed with your True Angle® tool, then get the miter angle from the Miter Table©.

The Miter Table© is also for cutting crown molding using a miter saw. Place the crown upside down (bottom of crown against the fence) for horizontal turns (horizontal ceilings), or the bottom of the crown on the saw table for vertical turns (cathedral ceilings). See Chapter 3 for more information on how to use the Miter Table©

Miter Table©

Corner Angle Inside or Outside	Miter Angle	Corner Angle Inside or Outside	Miter Angle	Corner Angle Inside or Outside	Miter Angle	Corner Angle Inside or Outside	Miter Angle
0 or 360	90.0	46 or 314	67.0	91 or 269	44.5	136 or 224	22.0
1 or 359	89.5	47 or 313	66.5	92 or 268	44.0	137 or 223	21.5
2 or 358	89.0	48 or 312	66.0	93 or 267	43.5	138 or 222	21.0
3 or 357	88.5	49 or 311	65.5	94 or 266	43.0	139 or 221	20.5
4 or 356	88.0	50 or 310	65.0	95 or 265	42.5	140 or 220	20.0
5 or 355	87.5	51 or 309	64.5	96 or 264	42.0	141 or 219	19.5
6 or 354	87.0	52 or 308	64.0	97 or 263	41.5	142 or 218	19.0
7 or 353	86.5	53 or 307	63.5	98 or 262	41.0	143 or 217	18.5
8 or 352	86.0	54 or 306	63.0	99 or 261	40.5	144 or 216	18.0
9 or 351	85.5	55 or 305	62.5	100 or 260	40.0	145 or 215	17.5
10 or 350	85.0	56 or 304	62.0	101 or 259	39.5	146 or 214	17.0
11 or 349	84.5	57 or 303	61.5	102 or 258	39.0	147 or 213	16.5
12 or 348	84.0	58 or 302	61.0	103 or 257	38.5	148 or 212	16.0
13 or 347	83.5	59 or 301	60.5	104 or 256	38.0	149 or 211	15.5
14 or 346	83.0	60 or 300	60.0	105 or 255	37.5	150 or 210	15.0
15 or 345	82.5	61 or 299	59.5	106 or 254	37.0	151 or 209	14.5
16 or 344	82.0	62 or 298	59.0	107 or 253	36.5	152 or 208	14.0
17 or 343	81.5	63 or 297	58.5	108 or 252	36.0	153 or 207	13.5
18 or 342	81.0	64 or 296	58.0	109 or 251	35.5	154 or 206	13.0
19 or 341	80.5	65 or 295	57.5	110 or 250	35.0	155 or 205	12.5
20 or 340	80.0	66 or 294	57.0	111 or 249	34.5	156 or 204	12.0
21 or 339	79.5	67 or 293	56.5	112 or 248	34.0	157 or 203	11.5
22 or 338	79.0	68 or 292	56.0	113 or 247	33.5	158 or 202	11.0
23 or 337	78.5	69 or 291	55.5	114 or 246	33.0	159 or 201	10.5
24 or 336	78.0	70 or 290	55.0	115 or 245	32.5	160 or 200	10.0
25 or 335	77.5	71 or 289	54.5	116 or 244	32.0	161 or 199	9.5
26 or 334	77.0	72 or 288	54.0	117 or 243	31.5	162 or 198	9.0
27 or 333	76.5	73 or 287	53.5	118 or 242	31.0	163 or 197	8.5
28 or 332	76.0	74 or 286	53.0	119 or 241	30.5	164 or 196	8.0
29 or 331	75.5	75 or 285	52.5	120 or 240	30.0	165 or 195	7.5
30 or 330	75.0	76 or 284	52.0	121 or 239	29.5	166 or 194	7.0
31 or 329	74.5	77 or 283	51.5	122 or 238	29.0	167 or 193	6.5
32 or 328	74.0	78 or 282	51.0	123 or 237	28.5	168 or 192	6.0
33 or 327	73.5	79 or 281	50.5	124 or 236	28.0	169 or 191	5.5
34 or 326	73.0	80 or 280	50.0	125 or 235	27.5	170 or 190	5.0
35 or 325	72.5	81 or 279	49.5	126 or 234	27.0	171 or 189	4.5
36 or 324	72.0	82 or 278	49.0	127 or 233	26.5	172 or 188	4.0
37 or 323	71.5	83 or 277	48.5	128 or 232	26.0	173 or 187	3.5
38 or 322	71.0	84 or 276	48.0	129 or 231	25.5	174 or 186	3.0
39 or 321	70.5	85 or 275	47.5	130 or 230	25.0	175 or 185	2.5
40 or 320	70.0	86 or 274	47.0	131 or 229	24.5	176 or 184	2.0
41 or 319	69.5	87 or 273	46.5	132 or 228	24.0	177 or 183	1.5
42 or 318	69.0	88 or 272	46.0	133 or 227	23.5	178 or 182	1.0
43 or 317	68.5	89 or 271	45.5	134 or 226	23.0	179 or 181	0.5
44 or 316	68.0	90 or 270	45.0	135 or 225	22.5	180 or 180	0.0
45 or 315	67.5	a Quint Group company		www.compoundmiter.com			

Crown Molding Table©

This table is for use with a <u>compound miter saw</u>, crown placed flat and face up. For a <u>miter saw</u>, you will need our **Miter Table©**. **Crown Slope Angle** is the angle between the back of the crown (when installed) and the plane in which you are turning the crown. Example: For 52°/38° crown turning in a horizontal plane (standard horizontal ceiling), the crown slope angle is 52°. For 52°/38° crown turning in a vertical plane (cathedral ceiling application), the crown slope angle is 38°. For 45°/45° crown, the crown slope angle is 45° (horizontal or vertical turns).

52°/38° Crown

Corner Angle	Crown Slope Angle						Corner Angle	Crown Slope Angle					
	52°		45°		38°			52°		45°		38°	
Inside or Outside	Miter Angle	Blade Tilt	Miter Angle	Blade Tilt	Miter Angle	Blade Tilt	Inside or Outside	Miter Angle	Blade Tilt	Miter Angle	Blade Tilt	Miter Angle	Blade Tilt
0 or 360	90.0	52.0	90.0	45.0	90.0	38.0	46 or 314	55.4	46.5	59.0	40.6	61.7	34.5
1 or 359	89.2	52.0	89.3	45.0	89.4	38.0	47 or 313	54.8	46.3	58.4	40.4	61.1	34.4
2 or 358	88.4	52.0	88.6	45.0	88.7	38.0	48 or 312	54.1	46.0	57.8	40.2	60.5	34.2
3 or 357	87.6	52.0	87.9	45.0	88.1	38.0	49 or 311	53.5	45.8	57.2	40.0	60.0	34.1
4 or 356	86.8	52.0	87.2	45.0	87.5	38.0	50 or 310	52.9	45.6	56.6	39.9	59.4	33.9
5 or 355	85.9	51.9	86.5	44.9	86.8	38.0	51 or 309	52.2	45.3	56.0	39.7	58.8	33.8
6 or 354	85.1	51.9	85.8	44.9	86.2	37.9	52 or 308	51.6	45.1	55.4	39.5	58.2	33.6
7 or 353	84.3	51.9	85.1	44.9	85.6	37.9	53 or 307	51.0	44.8	54.8	39.3	57.7	33.4
8 or 352	83.5	51.8	84.4	44.9	84.9	37.9	54 or 306	50.4	44.6	54.2	39.1	57.1	33.3
9 or 351	82.7	51.8	83.6	44.8	84.3	37.9	55 or 305	49.8	44.3	53.6	38.8	56.6	33.1
10 or 350	81.9	51.7	82.9	44.8	83.7	37.8	56 or 304	49.2	44.1	53.1	38.6	56.0	32.9
11 or 349	81.1	51.7	82.2	44.7	83.0	37.8	57 or 303	48.6	43.8	52.5	38.4	55.4	32.8
12 or 348	80.3	51.6	81.5	44.7	82.4	37.8	58 or 302	48.0	43.6	51.9	38.2	54.9	32.6
13 or 347	79.5	51.5	80.8	44.6	81.8	37.7	59 or 301	47.4	43.3	51.3	38.0	54.3	32.4
14 or 346	78.7	51.5	80.1	44.6	81.1	37.7	60 or 300	46.8	43.0	50.8	37.8	53.8	32.2
15 or 345	77.9	51.4	79.5	44.5	80.5	37.6	61 or 299	46.3	42.8	50.2	37.5	53.2	32.0
16 or 344	77.1	51.3	78.8	44.4	79.9	37.6	62 or 298	45.7	42.5	49.6	37.3	52.7	31.9
17 or 343	76.4	51.2	78.1	44.4	79.3	37.5	63 or 297	45.1	42.2	49.1	37.1	52.1	31.7
18 or 342	75.6	51.1	77.4	44.3	78.6	37.5	64 or 296	44.6	41.9	48.5	36.8	51.6	31.5
19 or 341	74.8	51.0	76.7	44.2	78.0	37.4	65 or 295	44.0	41.7	48.0	36.6	51.0	31.3
20 or 340	74.0	50.9	76.0	44.1	77.4	37.3	66 or 294	43.5	41.4	47.4	36.4	50.5	31.1
21 or 339	73.2	50.8	75.3	44.0	76.8	37.3	67 or 293	42.9	41.1	46.9	36.1	50.0	30.9
22 or 338	72.5	50.7	74.6	44.0	76.1	37.2	68 or 292	42.4	40.8	46.4	35.9	49.4	30.7
23 or 337	71.7	50.6	73.9	43.9	75.5	37.1	69 or 291	41.9	40.5	45.8	35.6	48.9	30.5
24 or 336	71.0	50.4	73.3	43.8	74.9	37.0	70 or 290	41.3	40.2	45.3	35.4	48.4	30.3
25 or 335	70.2	50.3	72.6	43.7	74.3	36.9	71 or 289	40.8	39.9	44.8	35.1	47.8	30.1
26 or 334	69.4	50.2	71.9	43.5	73.7	36.9	72 or 288	40.3	39.6	44.2	34.9	47.3	29.9
27 or 333	68.7	50.0	71.2	43.4	73.1	36.8	73 or 287	39.8	39.3	43.7	34.6	46.8	29.7
28 or 332	68.0	49.9	70.6	43.3	72.4	36.7	74 or 286	39.2	39.0	43.2	34.4	46.3	29.5
29 or 331	67.2	49.7	69.9	43.2	71.8	36.6	75 or 285	38.7	38.7	42.7	34.1	45.8	29.2
30 or 330	66.5	49.6	69.2	43.1	71.2	36.5	76 or 284	38.2	38.4	42.1	33.9	45.2	29.0
31 or 329	65.8	49.4	68.6	43.0	70.6	36.4	77 or 283	37.7	38.1	41.6	33.6	44.7	28.8
32 or 328	65.0	49.2	67.9	42.8	70.0	36.3	78 or 282	37.2	37.8	41.1	33.3	44.2	28.6
33 or 327	64.3	49.1	67.3	42.7	69.4	36.2	79 or 281	36.8	37.4	40.6	33.1	43.7	28.4
34 or 326	63.6	48.9	66.6	42.5	68.8	36.1	80 or 280	36.3	37.1	40.1	32.8	43.2	28.1
35 or 325	62.9	48.7	66.0	42.4	68.2	36.0	81 or 279	35.8	36.8	39.6	32.5	42.7	27.9
36 or 324	62.2	48.5	65.3	42.3	67.6	35.8	82 or 278	35.3	36.5	39.1	32.3	42.2	27.7
37 or 323	61.5	48.4	64.7	42.1	67.0	35.7	83 or 277	34.8	36.2	38.6	32.0	41.7	27.5
38 or 322	60.8	48.2	64.0	42.0	66.4	35.6	84 or 276	34.4	35.8	38.1	31.7	41.2	27.2
39 or 321	60.1	48.0	63.4	41.8	65.8	35.5	85 or 275	33.9	35.5	37.7	31.4	40.7	27.0
40 or 320	59.4	47.8	62.8	41.6	65.2	35.3	86 or 274	33.4	35.2	37.2	31.1	40.2	26.8
41 or 319	58.7	47.6	62.1	41.5	64.6	35.2	87 or 273	33.0	34.9	36.7	30.9	39.7	26.5
42 or 318	58.1	47.4	61.5	41.3	64.0	35.1	88 or 272	32.5	34.5	36.2	30.6	39.2	26.3
43 or 317	57.4	47.2	60.9	41.1	63.4	34.9	89 or 271	32.1	34.2	35.7	30.3	38.7	26.0
44 or 316	56.7	46.9	60.3	41.0	62.9	34.8	90 or 270	31.6	33.9	35.3	30.0	38.2	25.8
45 or 315	56.1	46.7	59.6	40.8	62.3	34.7	www.compoundmiter.com						

Corner Angle is the measured angle of the corner. Use your True Angle® tool to measure the true corner angle formed by the crown molding. Find your measured corner angle in the Crown Molding Table© and read across to the right to get the miter and blade tilt angles for the crown slope angle you have. (0° miter is a square cut, 0° blade tilt is a vertical blade). For all of the latest, visit us @ **www.compoundmiter.com,** a Quint Group company.

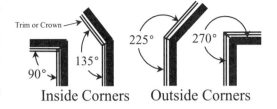

Inside Corners   Outside Corners

Crown Molding Table©

| Corner Angle | Crown Slope Angle | | | | | | Corner Angle | Crown Slope Angle | | | | | |
| | 52° | | 45° | | 38° | | | 52° | | 45° | | 38° | |
Inside or Outside	Miter Angle	Blade Tilt	Miter Angle	Blade Tilt	Miter Angle	Blade Tilt	Inside or Outside	Miter Angle	Blade Tilt	Miter Angle	Blade Tilt	Miter Angle	Blade Tilt
91 or 269	31.2	33.5	34.8	29.7	37.8	25.6	136 or 224	14.0	17.2	15.9	15.4	17.7	13.3
92 or 268	30.7	33.2	34.3	29.4	37.3	25.3	137 or 223	13.6	16.8	15.6	15.0	17.2	13.0
93 or 267	30.3	32.8	33.9	29.1	36.8	25.1	138 or 222	13.3	16.4	15.2	14.7	16.8	12.7
94 or 266	29.9	32.5	33.4	28.8	36.3	24.8	139 or 221	13.0	16.0	14.8	14.3	16.4	12.5
95 or 265	29.4	32.2	32.9	28.5	35.8	24.6	140 or 220	12.6	15.6	14.4	14.0	16.0	12.2
96 or 264	29.0	31.8	32.5	28.2	35.4	24.3	141 or 219	12.3	15.3	14.1	13.7	15.6	11.9
97 or 263	28.6	31.5	32.0	27.9	34.9	24.1	142 or 218	12.0	14.9	13.7	13.3	15.2	11.6
98 or 262	28.2	31.1	31.6	27.6	34.4	23.8	143 or 217	11.6	14.5	13.3	13.0	14.8	11.3
99 or 261	27.7	30.8	31.1	27.3	33.9	23.6	144 or 216	11.3	14.1	12.9	12.6	14.4	11.0
100 or 260	27.3	30.4	30.7	27.0	33.5	23.3	145 or 215	11.0	13.7	12.6	12.3	14.0	10.7
101 or 259	26.9	30.1	30.2	26.7	33.0	23.1	146 or 214	10.7	13.3	12.2	11.9	13.5	10.4
102 or 258	26.5	29.7	29.8	26.4	32.5	22.8	147 or 213	10.3	12.9	11.8	11.6	13.1	10.1
103 or 257	26.1	29.4	29.4	26.1	32.1	22.5	148 or 212	10.0	12.5	11.5	11.2	12.7	9.8
104 or 256	25.7	29.0	28.9	25.8	31.6	22.3	149 or 211	9.7	12.2	11.1	10.9	12.3	9.5
105 or 255	25.3	28.7	28.5	25.5	31.2	22.0	150 or 210	9.4	11.8	10.7	10.5	11.9	9.2
106 or 254	24.9	28.3	28.1	25.2	30.7	21.7	151 or 209	9.0	11.4	10.4	10.2	11.5	8.9
107 or 253	24.5	28.0	27.6	24.9	30.2	21.5	152 or 208	8.7	11.0	10.0	9.8	11.1	8.6
108 or 252	24.1	27.6	27.2	24.6	29.8	21.2	153 or 207	8.4	10.6	9.6	9.5	10.7	8.3
109 or 251	23.7	27.2	26.8	24.2	29.3	20.9	154 or 206	8.1	10.2	9.3	9.2	10.3	8.0
110 or 250	23.3	26.9	26.3	23.9	28.9	20.7	155 or 205	7.8	9.8	8.9	8.8	9.9	7.7
111 or 249	22.9	26.5	25.9	23.6	28.4	20.4	156 or 204	7.5	9.4	8.5	8.5	9.5	7.4
112 or 248	22.6	26.1	25.5	23.3	28.0	20.1	157 or 203	7.1	9.0	8.2	8.1	9.1	7.1
113 or 247	22.2	25.8	25.1	23.0	27.5	19.9	158 or 202	6.8	8.6	7.8	7.8	8.7	6.7
114 or 246	21.8	25.4	24.7	22.7	27.1	19.6	159 or 201	6.5	8.3	7.5	7.4	8.3	6.4
115 or 245	21.4	25.0	24.3	22.3	26.7	19.3	160 or 200	6.2	7.9	7.1	7.1	7.9	6.1
116 or 244	21.0	24.7	23.8	22.0	26.2	19.0	161 or 199	5.9	7.5	6.7	6.7	7.5	5.8
117 or 243	20.7	24.3	23.4	21.7	25.8	18.8	162 or 198	5.6	7.1	6.4	6.4	7.1	5.5
118 or 242	20.3	23.9	23.0	21.4	25.3	18.5	163 or 197	5.3	6.7	6.0	6.0	6.7	5.2
119 or 241	19.9	23.6	22.6	21.0	24.9	18.2	164 or 196	4.9	6.3	5.7	5.6	6.3	4.9
120 or 240	19.6	23.2	22.2	20.7	24.5	17.9	165 or 195	4.6	5.9	5.3	5.3	5.9	4.6
121 or 239	19.2	22.8	21.8	20.4	24.0	17.6	166 or 194	4.3	5.5	5.0	4.9	5.5	4.3
122 or 238	18.8	22.5	21.4	20.0	23.6	17.4	167 or 193	4.0	5.1	4.6	4.6	5.1	4.0
123 or 237	18.5	22.1	21.0	19.7	23.2	17.1	168 or 192	3.7	4.7	4.3	4.2	4.7	3.7
124 or 236	18.1	21.7	20.6	19.4	22.7	16.8	169 or 191	3.4	4.3	3.9	3.9	4.3	3.4
125 or 235	17.8	21.3	20.2	19.1	22.3	16.5	170 or 190	3.1	3.9	3.5	3.5	3.9	3.1
126 or 234	17.4	21.0	19.8	18.7	21.9	16.2	171 or 189	2.8	3.5	3.2	3.2	3.5	2.8
127 or 233	17.1	20.6	19.4	18.4	21.4	15.9	172 or 188	2.5	3.2	2.8	2.8	3.2	2.5
128 or 232	16.7	20.2	19.0	18.1	21.0	15.7	173 or 187	2.2	2.8	2.5	2.5	2.8	2.2
129 or 231	16.4	19.8	18.6	17.7	20.6	15.4	174 or 186	1.8	2.4	2.1	2.1	2.4	1.8
130 or 230	16.0	19.5	18.2	17.4	20.2	15.1	175 or 185	1.5	2.0	1.8	1.8	2.0	1.5
131 or 229	15.7	19.1	17.9	17.1	19.8	14.8	176 or 184	1.2	1.6	1.4	1.4	1.6	1.2
132 or 228	15.3	18.7	17.5	16.7	19.3	14.5	177 or 183	0.9	1.2	1.1	1.1	1.2	0.9
133 or 227	15.0	18.3	17.1	16.4	18.9	14.2	178 or 182	0.6	0.8	0.7	0.7	0.8	0.6
134 or 226	14.6	17.9	16.7	16.0	18.5	13.9	179 or 181	0.3	0.4	0.4	0.4	0.4	0.3
135 or 225	14.3	17.6	16.3	15.7	18.1	13.6	180 or 180	0.0	0.0	0.0	0.0	0.0	0.0
Quint Measuring Systems, Inc.							www.compoundmiter.com						

Compound Miter Chart©

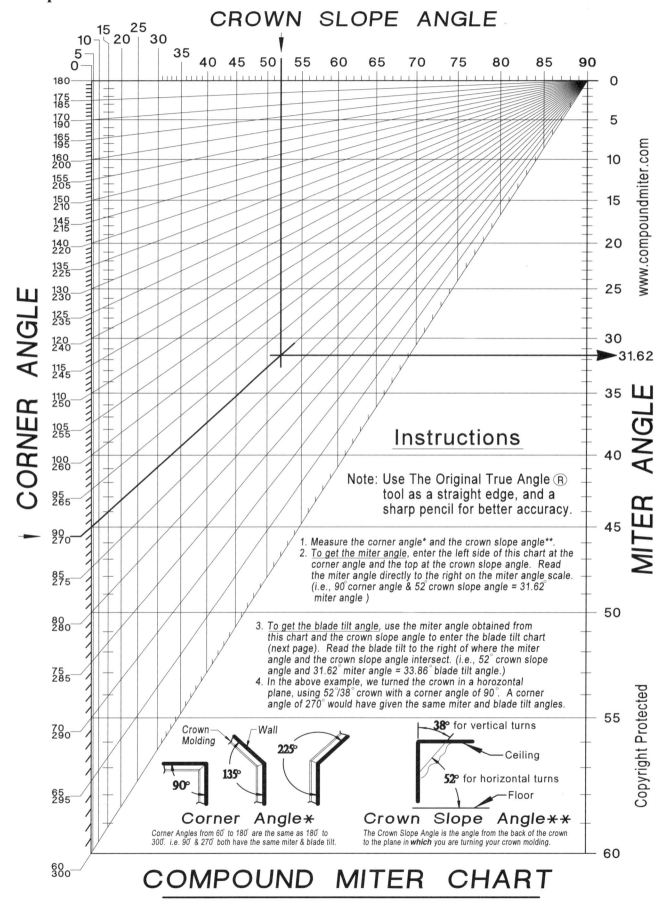

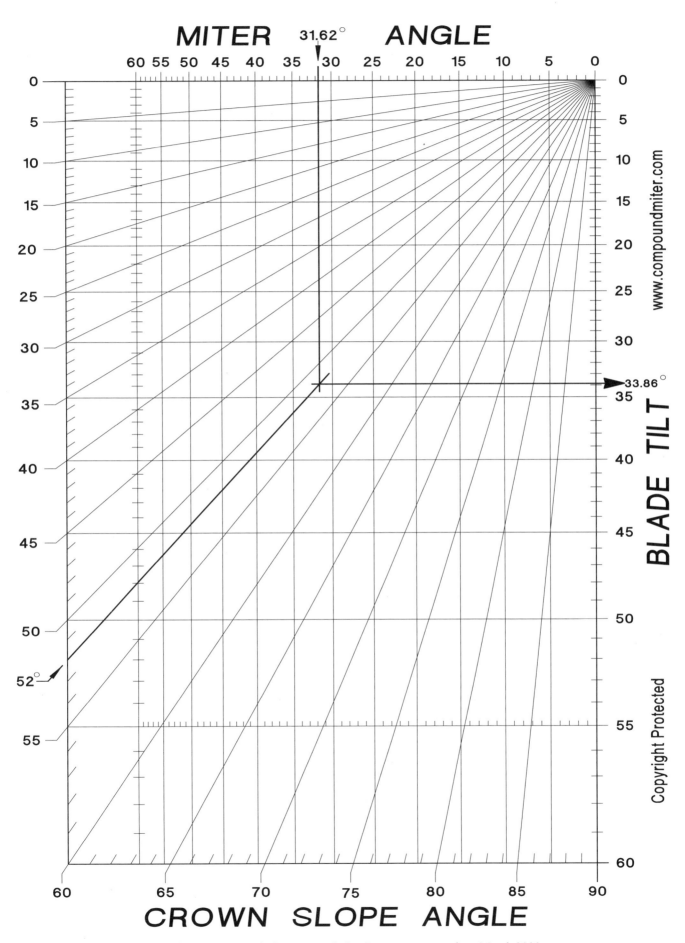

MITER 31.62° ANGLE

BLADE TILT 33.86°

52°

CROWN SLOPE ANGLE

www.compoundmiter.com

Copyright Protected

Conversion Table - Fractions to Inches

Use this table when you are making measurements and need to convert fractions of an inch to decimals of an inch. For example, if you measured a bullnose radius of 13/16", you would use 0.8125" as the radius for Table 2 (page 56).

Conversion Table
Fractions (inches) to Decimals (inches)

1/64 = 0.015625	11/32 = 0.343750	43/64 = 0.671875
1/32 = 0.031250	23/64 = 0.359375	11/16 = 0.687500
3/64 = 0.046875	3/8 = 0.375000	45/64 = 0.703125
1/16 = 0.062500	25/64 = 0.390625	23/32 = 0.718750
5/64 = 0.078125	13/32 = 0.406250	47/64 = 0.734375
3/32 = 0.093750	27/64 = 0.421875	3/4 = 0.750000
7/64 = 0.109375	7/16 = 0.437500	49/64 = 0.765625
1/8 = 0.125000	29/64 = 0.453125	25/32 = 0.781250
9/64 = 0.140625	15/32 = 0.468750	51/64 = 0.796875
5/32 = 0.156250	31/64 = 0.484375	13/16 = 0.812500
11/64 = 0.171875	1/2 = 0.500000	53/64 = 0.828125
3/16 = 0.187500	33/64 = 0.515625	27/32 = 0.843750
13/64 = 0.203125	17/32 = 0.531250	55/64 = 0.859375
7/32 = 0.218750	35/64 = 0.546875	7/8 = 0.875000
15/64 = 0.234375	9/16 = 0.562500	57/64 = 0.890625
1/4 = 0.250000	37/64 = 0.578125	29/32 = 0.906250
17/64 = 0.265625	19/32 = 0.593750	59/64 = 0.921875
9/32 = 0.281250	39/64 = 0.609375	15/16 = 0.937500
19/64 = 0.296875	5/8 = 0.625000	61/64 = 0.953125
5/16 = 0.312500	41/64 = 0.640625	31/32 = 0.968750
21/64 = 0.328125	21/32 = 0.656250	63/64 = 0.984375

Conversion Table - Rise/Run (Pitch) to Roof Slope (Degrees)

Pitch is defined as Rise ÷ Run and is usually expressed as so much rise (vertical length) for a certain run (horizontal length). Both of these measurements must be expressed in the same units (e.g., feet, inches, yards, etc.). You cannot use different units for rise and run. If your rise is in feet, the run *must* be expressed in feet. If the rise is in inches, the run *must* also be in inches.

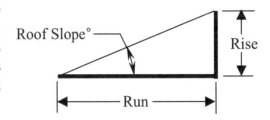

Below is a conversion table for the common expression with the run as 12 units. For example, a 4x12 (read as 4 on 12) pitch roof has a roof slope of 18 1/2°.

Degrees For 48 Different Pitches					
Degrees	**Pitch**	**Degrees**	**Pitch**	**Degrees**	**Pitch**
2 1/2 ° --	1/2 x 12	35 1/4 ° --	8 1/2 x 12	54 ° --	16 1/2 x 12
4 3/4 ° --	1 x 12	36 3/4 ° --	9 x 12	54 3/4 ° --	17 x 12
7 1/4 ° --	1 1/2 x 12	38 1/4 ° --	9 1/2 x 12	55 1/2 ° --	17 1/2 x 12
9 1/2 ° --	2 x 12	39 3/4 ° --	10 x 12	56 1/4 ° --	18 x 12
11 3/4 ° --	2 1/2 x 12	41 1/4 ° --	10 1/2 x 12	57 ° --	18 1/2 x 12
14 ° --	3 x 12	42 1/2 ° --	11 x 12	57 3/4 ° --	19 x 12
16 1/4 ° --	3 1/2 x 12	43 3/4 ° --	11 1/2 x 12	58 1/2 ° --	19 1/2 x 12
18 1/2 ° --	4 x 12	45 ° --	12 x 12	59 ° --	20 x 12
20 1/2 ° --	4 1/2 x 12	46 1/4 ° --	12 1/2 x 12	59 3/4 ° --	20 1/2 x 12
22 1/2 ° --	5 x 12	47 1/4 ° --	13 x 12	60 1/4 ° --	21 x 12
24 1/2 ° --	5 1/2 x 12	48 1/4 ° --	13 1/2 x 12	60 3/4 ° --	21 1/2 x 12
26 1/2 ° --	6 x 12	49 1/2 ° --	14 x 12	61 1/2 ° --	22 x 12
28 1/2 ° --	6 1/2 x 12	50 1/2 ° --	14 1/2 x 12	62 ° --	22 1/2 x 12
30 1/4 ° --	7 x 12	51 1/4 ° --	15 x 12	62 1/2 ° --	23 x 12
32 ° --	7 1/2 x 12	52 1/4 ° --	15 1/2 x 12	63 ° --	23 1/2 x 12
33 3/4 ° --	8 x 12	53 1/4 ° --	16 x 12	63 1/2 ° --	24 x 12

To order products mentioned throughout this book, visit me online at http://www.compoundmiter.com or call our toll free number 866-544-2016 (within the 48 continental US), 8 a.m. – 5 p.m. Central, M-F.

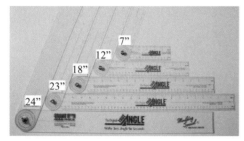

The *Original* True Angle® tools are a must. You need an accurate measurement of the corner angle where you will be installing your crown molding or trim in order to use the table and charts that are contained in this book. The True Angle® tools are also available in larger sizes ranging from 30" to 96" which are ideally suited for construction use.

The Exact Angle® squares are available in many shapes and sizes. Shown here are the setup and try squares. Also available are 22.5°, 30°, & 45° templates, double try squares, dovetail squares, miter squares, and center-finding rules. These are great for squaring your saws and for layout applications when fixed angles are required. The Exact Angle® squares are manufactured with the same precision and accuracy as the True Angle® tools, are unbreakable, and carry a lifetime warrantee.

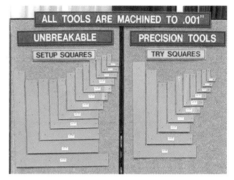

The Miter Excel Program© (immediate download available) will calculate the miter and/or blade tilt angles by simply typing in the desired corner angle and crown slope angle. This is especially useful when working with cathedral ceilings. You will also be able to input your information and get instant calculations for flowerpots or birdhouses. The Miter Excel Program© also contains the Miter Table©, Crown Molding Table©, and the Compound Miter Chart©. Note: You must have Microsoft Excel 97 or higher installed on your computer to run this program.

Crown molding templates are essential to prevent you from cutting your crown molding incorrectly. I have provided simple instructions in this book for you to make your own templates. If you would rather purchase a set, I have made these available to you.

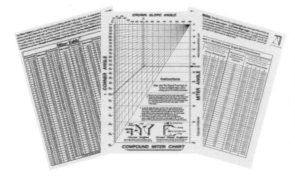

I have taken the Miter Table©, Crown Molding Table© and the Compound Miter Chart© and printed them on heavyweight paper and laminated both sides with 5mil plastic. These are ideal to keep with your saw for quick reference. If these get wet or soiled, you need only wipe them clean and they are as good as new.

Thank you for purchasing Crown Molding & Trim: Install It Like A PRO! You will find my book to be the only truly do-it-yourself handbook for cutting crown molding and/or trim available on the market today. Master any compound miter angle. If you can hammer a nail, you can install crown molding and trim like a pro!

Sincerely

C. Wayne Drake

Wayne@CompoundMiter.com

Notes

Notes

Notes

Notes